WORLD WAR II
FROM ORIGINAL SOURCES

THE NORMANDY CAMPAIGN 1944

BOB CARRUTHERS

Pen & Sword
MILITARY

This edition published in 2012 by
Pen & Sword Military
An imprint of
Pen & Sword Books Ltd
47 Church Street
Barnsley
South Yorkshire
S70 2AS

First published in Great Britain in 2012 in digital format by
Coda Books Ltd.

ISBN 978 1 78159 141 3

The right of Bob Carruthers to be identified as Author of this work has been
asserted by him in accordance with the Copyright, Designs and Patents Act 1988.

A CIP catalogue record for this book is
available from the British Library

Printed and bound by
CPI Group (UK) Ltd, Croydon, CR0 4YY

Pen & Sword Books Ltd incorporates the Imprints of Pen & Sword Aviation, Pen
& Sword Family History, Pen & Sword Maritime, Pen & Sword Military, Pen
& Sword Discovery, Pen & Sword Politics, Pen & Sword Atlas, Pen & Sword
Archaeology, Wharncliffe Local History, Wharncliffe True Crime, Wharncliffe
Transport, Pen & Sword Select, Pen & Sword Military Classics, Leo Cooper, The
Praetorian Press, Claymore Press, Remember When, Seaforth Publishing and
Frontline Publishing

For a complete list of Pen & Sword titles please contact
PEN & SWORD BOOKS LIMITED
47 Church Street, Barnsley, South Yorkshire, S70 2AS, England
E-mail: enquiries@pen-and-sword.co.uk
Website: www.pen-and-sword.co.uk

CONTENTS

- CHAPTER 1 -
THE DRESS REHEARSAL

When Stalin sat down to write to Winston Churchill on July 18th 1941, the Second World War had reached its darkest hour. Russian forces were in headlong retreat and the British were struggling to hold the tide of German advances in the western desert. *"It seems to me that the military situation of the Soviet Union as well as of Great Britain would be considerably improved if there could be established a front against Hitler in the West,"* wrote Stalin. Fortunately for the Allies there was one glimmer of hope on the horizon, but it would not arrive until later in that fateful year. The long awaited US intervention had so far failed to materialise, as strong political forces within the USA kept America out of the war.

Despite the fact that President Roosevelt was increasingly a hawk in military matters, by late 1941 US participation was still by no means certain. Stalin, therefore, must have been overjoyed when, in December 1941, Hitler shocked the world with his declaration of war on the United States. This unexpected and, it should be said, uncharacteristic declaration of war before taking military action, dragged the US into the war by virtue of Hitler's most perverse decision in a career of perverse decisions. By declaring war on the largest industrial nation on earth, he signed his own death warrant, but it would take some time before the sentence could be carried out.

From the moment Hitler declared war on America, there did at last begin to be a genuine possibility that Stalin's much hoped for 'Second Front' would actually arise within a realistic time frame. Nonetheless, there was still a considerable deal of resistance to overcome within the US. George C. Marshall, the US Army Chief of Staff, desperately needed action to justify his *'Germany First'* policy, at a time when the bulk of public opinion in the US still favoured the Pacific war as a priority. Ultimately, Marshall triumphed and a massive build up of US troops in Britain began from 1942 onwards, with an eye towards the early invasion of continental Europe. In reality, however, there was no realistic prospect of an invasion as early as 1942.

THE SECOND FRONT

With Stalin increasingly vocal in his demands for a Second Front, Churchill had to sanction Allied action in France. In order to demonstrate the magnitude of the task, but still give the impression that Britain was not entirely impotent, as well as to prepare for the day when British forces would be required to stage a full scale invasion of the Continent, a large attack was planned against the German held town of Dieppe.

The disastrous raid on Dieppe in August 1942 would prove just how far the Allies had to go before they could begin to contemplate a serious attack on mainland Europe.

British troops rehearsing for the coming attack on Fortress Europe during 1942. Here, Sir Gerald Bernard Paget is seen aboard a British Crusader tank. The Crusader was one of many British models which failed to reach the quality threshold, and was withdrawn from service before the Normandy invasion.

Dieppe has been described variously as a 'Raid', a 'Combined Operation', and 'a Reconnaissance in Force'. The last is probably the best description.

The first plans for the attack were laid in the month of April and a number of ports on the French coast were carefully studied as possible objectives before Dieppe was finally selected. It should be recognised that the Allies were not looking for soft spots; they were *"aiming to trade blows with the enemy"* in order to gauge the strength of the German defences.

THE CANADIANS

As soon as the outline plan was ready it was placed before the Chiefs of Staff Committee. Once approval was received, the next step was to choose the troops for the undertaking. After much deliberation the Canadians, many of whom had been waiting impatiently for

The construction of the Atlantic Wall was a massive undertaking which was designed to fortify the whole coast of occupied Europe from Norway to Spain. Obviously an undertaking of this scale could never be realistically completed, but the beaches which were most under threat were the first to receive attention.

A German sentry guards part of the Atlantic wall defences. This picture was taken on the French coast, probably during 1942.

HANDBOOK ON GERMAN MILITARY FORCES
EXTRACT NO.1

GERMAN NATIONAL CHARACTERISTICS

"......an outstanding char-acteristic of the German nation is its fondness for everything connected with militarism.

The Germans believe that only the offensive can achieve success on the field, particularly when combined with the element of surprise. German military literature, for the past century, has emphasised the need for aggressiveness in all military operations.

The Germans have been thoroughly aware of the psychological component in warfare and have developed systematic terrorisation to a high degree.

At the same time they have placed considerable reliance on novel and sensational weapons such as the mass use of armour, the robot bomb, and the super-heavy tank. Their principal weaknesses in this regard have been their failure to integrate these new techniques with established arms and tactics. German field artillery, for example, did not maintain pace with German armour and their devotion to automatic weapons at the expense of accuracy.

A highly trained officer corps and a thoroughly disciplined army are the necessary elements to implement this aggressive philosophy. German tactical doctrines stress the responsibility and the initiative of subordinates. The belief of former years that the German Army was inflexible and lacking in initiative has been completely destroyed in this war, in which aggressive and daring leadership has been responsible for many bold decisions. Yet, while the Germans have many excellent tacticians, they tend to repeat the same type of manoeuvres, a fact which has been fully exploited by Allied commanders.

RECENT TACTICAL TRENDS

From the time when the German Army was forced on the defensive by the Allied armies, German tactical doctrines have undergone modifications such as renunciation (except in unstated instances) of air support, and the substitution of linear defence for elastic offensive defence.

The primary goal of Germany today is to gain time and to achieve victory in a political sense, since the Germans are no longer capable of a military victory. Of necessity their military operations now supplement this effort and have become a large-scale delaying action.

EXERCISE OF COMMAND

The U. S. and German doctrines applied in exercise of the command are virtually identical. The Germans stress the necessity of the staff in assisting the commander to evaluate the situation and in preparing and disseminating orders to the lower units. They emphasise that the commander should be well forward with his units not only for the purpose of facilitating communication, but also because his presence has a salutary effect on the troops....."

This is the first extract from the 1945 manual, 'Handbook on German Military Forces', issued to US troops destined to fight in Europe. As such, it provides an interesting primary source on the German forces as viewed through Allied eyes. It is also a good guide to just how well-informed and accurate Allied intelligence was in the latter stages of World War Two. Further extracts appear throughout the book.

more than two years for the chance to see some action, were finally granted their wish. Before it was finally agreed, however, that they should be employed, the General Officer commanding the First Canadian Army, Lieutenant-General McNaughton, studied the plan and satisfied himself that the objectives were worthwhile and that the means available were likely to be adequate for the task in hand. That task was to probe into German-held territory and test the strength of the defences.

While the Force Commanders at Combined Operations Headquarters developed the final plan in the most elaborate detail, the troops were being prepared. Naturally, they were in complete ignorance of the task before them but, as one officer reported, *"there was something in the air that seemed to give them a fresh enthusiasm."* Twice they carried out full-dress rehearsals of the actual attack while staff officers anxiously checked times and synchronisation.

German coastal defence troops on an exercise march past under the watchful presence of an anti-aircraft gun.

Wrecked Allied landing craft in the aftermath of the failed raid on Dieppe.

The Canadian military force involved was composed basically of large elements of a Canadian Division and a battalion of the 1st Canadian Army Tank Brigade. With them were the 3rd, 4th and Royal Marine 'A' Commandos and small detachments of United States Rangers and Fighting French troops.

The naval force had no vessels larger than destroyers and for the most part consisted of landing craft of various types and support craft.

PROVOKING A REACTION

In many respects the Dieppe raid turned military logic on its head. While surprise was an important element of the initial assault, it was actually hoped that the Germans would react strongly to the attack, not only on the ground but also in the air, and the RAF prepared for a major battle. Air units were drawn from all operational commands of the Air Force and these were joined by Canadian, American, New Zealand, Polish, Czech, Norwegian, Belgian and French squadrons.

In the early hours of the morning of August 19th, minesweeping flotillas led an armada of more than two hundred vessels towards the French coast. Every possible precaution had been taken to maintain secrecy, because surprise was all-important to the venture.

The number one objective of the raid was of course Dieppe itself, but the Germans had the town and its seaward approaches covered by a number of batteries on the cliff top to left and right. These included two heavy batteries between four and five miles away on each side of Dieppe, located at Berneval and Varengeville respectively. If these remained in action they would be able to pour damaging fire onto the Canadian forces both in the town and off-shore. The Commandos, therefore, were given the task of silencing them. No. 4 Commando, led by Lieutenant-Colonel Lord Lovat, had the right flank (Varengeville), and No. 3 Commando, under Lieutenant-Colonel Durnford Slater, had Berneval as their objective.

Lieutenant-Colonel Lord Lovat comparing notes with another officer on their return from the Dieppe raid.

HANDBOOK ON GERMAN MILITARY FORCES
EXTRACT NO.2

OPERATIONAL RECONNAISSANCE

".....operational reconnaissance, penetrating over a large area in great depth, provides the basis for strategic planning and action. This type of reconnaissance is intended to determine the location and activities of enemy forces, particularly localities of rail concentrations, forward or rearward displacements of personnel, loading or unloading areas of army elements, the construction of field or permanent fortifications, and hostile air force concentrations. Identification of large enemy motorised elements, especially on an open flank, is important. Operational reconnaissance is carried out by the Air Force and by motorised units. Aerial photography units operate at altitudes of 16,500 to 26,500 feet. Since missions assigned to operational air reconnaissance units are generally limited to the observation of important roads and railroads, reconnaissance sectors and areas normally are not assigned. The motorised units employed for operational reconnaissance have only directions and objectives assigned.

TACTICAL RECONNAISSANCE

PURPOSE
Tactical reconnaissance, carried out in the area behind the operational reconnaissance, provides the basis for the commitment of troops. Its mission embraces identification of the enemy's organisation, disposition, strength, and antiaircraft defence; determination of the enemy's

reinforcement capabilities; and terrain reconnaissance of advanced sectors. Air Force reconnaissance units and motorised and mounted reconnaissance battalions are employed for tactical reconnaissance. Their direction and radius of employment are based upon the results of the operational reconnaissance.

AIR RECONNAISSANCE

Tactical air reconnaissance is normally made from altitudes of 6,500 to 16,000 feet. As a rule, air reconnaissance units are assigned specific reconnaissance areas, the boundaries of which normally do not coincide with sectors assigned to ground units. Reconnaissance planes generally are employed singly.

The German army placed a great deal of emphasis on individual initiative. Decision making was pushed as far down the hierarchy as possible and junior officers were expected to take on a number of tasks which were reserved for officers much higher up the command chain in the Allied armies.

GROUND RECONNAISSANCE

Sectors of responsibility are assigned to ground tactical reconnaissance battalions. In order to make them independent or to facilitate their change of direction, battalions may be assigned only reconnaissance objectives. In such instances,

An SS Unterschafuhrer (the equivalent of a senior corporal), these men were capable of leading and inspiring their men to remarkable feats of arms.

Although the Panzer divisions were relatively well equipped and highly mechanised, the German army as a whole, even in 1944, was less mechanised than the British army had been for the campaign in France in 1940.

boundary lines separate adjacent units. The Germans avoid using main roads as boundary lines, defining the sectors in such a way that main roads fall within the reconnaissance sectors. The width of a sector is determined by the situation, the type and strength of the reconnaissance battalion, the road net, and the terrain. In general, the width of a sector assigned to a motorised reconnaissance battalion does not exceed 30 miles.

TACTICAL RECONNAISSANCE PROCEDURES

When a motorised reconnaissance column expects contact with the enemy, it advances by bounds. The length of bounds depends on the cover the terrain offers as well as on the road net. As the distance from the enemy decreases, the bounds are shortened. The Germans utilise roads as long as possible and usually use different routes for the advance and the return.

The reconnaissance battalion commander normally sends out patrols which advance by bounds. Their distance in front of the battalion depends on the situation, the terrain, and the range of the signal equipment, but as a rule they are not more than an hour's travelling distance (about 25 miles) ahead of the battalion. The battalion serves as the reserve for the patrols and as an advance message centre (Meldekopf), collecting the messages and relaying them to the rear. Armoured reconnaissance cars, armoured half-tracks, or motorcycles compose the motorised reconnaissance patrols, whose exact composition depends on their mission and on the situation. Motorcycles are used to fill in gaps and intervals, thereby thickening the reconnaissance net.

When the proximity of the enemy does not permit profitable employment of the motorised reconnaissance battalion, it is withdrawn and the motorised elements of the divisional reconnaissance battalion take over.

Divisional reconnaissance battalions seldom operate more than one day's march (18 miles) in front of the division, covering an area approximately 6 miles wide....."

The MG42 medium machine gun was a fearsome weapon with a tremendously high rate of fire. It was, however, prone to jam and required a great deal of maintenance.

THE DIEPPE RAID

The Allied plan for the raid on Dieppe envisaged a strong attack by armoured forces and infantry in the centre, supported by commando attacks on both flanks. This was to prove a miniature rehearsal of the D-Day plan in 1944, when the commando forces were replaced by paratroop drops on the flanks.

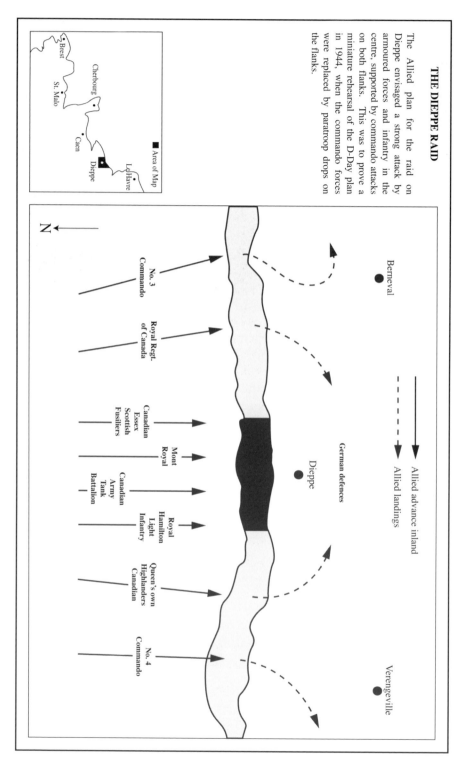

Brest

Cherbourg

St. Malo

Caen

Dieppe

Le Havre

■ Area of Map

N ←

Berneval

No. 3 Commando

Royal Regt. of Canada

Canadian Essex Scottish Fusiliers

Mont Royal

Canadian Army Tank Battalion

German defences

Dieppe

Royal Hamilton Light Infantry

Queen's own Highlanders Canadian

No. 4 Commando

Verengeville

Allied advance inland

Allied landings

Britain's Minister of Defence and his Chief-of-Staff. Responsibility for Britain's defence was largely the task of these four British leaders, seen here in the gardens of Number 10 Downing Street. Left to right are Air Chief Marshal Sir Charles Portal, General Sir Alan Brooke, Mr Winston Churchill, Prime Minister and Minister of Defence, and Admiral Sir Andrew Cunningham, First Sea Lord.

BAD LUCK AT SEA

At 3.47am a tragic misadventure befell the expedition. Only seven miles from the French coast the left flank of the force, which had moved into its assault positions, ran into a small convoy, consisting of a tanker and an armed escort. A minor battle developed which would have been of no real consequence if it had not robbed the attack of the element of surprise. In practice, this really affected only the left flanking forces, but in an operation with units as interdependent as they were at Dieppe, it was little short of disastrous. If No. 3 Commando, bound for Berneval, had not had this ill-fortune and been able to function with the same degree of success as No. 4 Commando on the right flank, the operation would have probably been much less costly. But these are the fortunes of war, and luck was certainly against the Canadians.

As a result of the unexpected sea conflict the landing craft carrying No. 3 Commando were scattered and many were damaged. Twenty-five minutes after they were due, six craft made a landing in broad daylight on one beach and one arrived at another beach. The larger section was met with murderous fire and although the men went forward, they were gradually overwhelmed by vastly superior forces. The smaller party consisted of Major Peter Young, two officers and seventeen men. Their arsenal consisted of ten rifles, a Bren gun, six Tommy guns, three pistols, two mortars and a few bombs. They knew that the battery they had to attack was manned by at least two hundred troops. Undeterred, they set out to find a way to the top of the cliff and from there to Berneval where the battery was located. A frontal attack was out of the question, so the Commando remnant determinedly sniped the garrison for nearly two hours, and caused so much harassment that, at one point, the Germans turned a 5.9 inch coastal defence gun on them at point-blank range. When their ammunition was exhausted and Young and

The agony of defeat can be seen on the face of the wounded man who is being helped by his colleagues in this still from a German newsreel, shot at the time of the Dieppe raid.

BATTLE RECONNAISSANCE PATROLS

"......the Germans send out reconnaissance patrols, consisting of a noncommissioned officer and three or four men, to get such information as the location of enemy positions and minefields. They generally avoid contact and retreat when fired on.

COMBAT PATROLS

These consist of at least one noncommissioned officer and eight men, but are usually much stronger. As a rule the combat patrol is commanded by a sergeant who has under him 15 to 20 men, organised in two equal sections, each commanded by a section leader. These are raiding patrols, and their mission often includes bringing back prisoners of war. Since Allied air supremacy has neutralised German air reconnaissance to a great extent, the Germans have placed increased importance on prisoners of war, especially officers, as a source of information on enemy strength, dispositions, and intentions.

Combat or other types of patrols are often sent out to test the strength of enemy outposts. If an outpost proves to be weakly held, the patrol attacks, occupies the position, and remains there until relieved by troops from the rear. If the patrol is strongly garrisoned, the patrol attempts to return with a prisoner of war.

TERRAIN RECONNAISSANCE

The Germans place great emphasis on terrain reconnaissance, realising the influence terrain has upon the conduct of operations. Most of their usual reconnaissance missions include terrain reconnaissance tasks. Terrain may be so important at times as to require reconnaissance by special units. Ground and air reconnaissance units give special attention to the road net, its density, condition, road blocks, mines, and demolitions, as well as to the terrain itself, particularly tank country.

EQUIPMENT AND SUPPORT

The Germans equip their ground battle-reconnaissance patrols with machine pistols and one or two light machine guns that are used to cover the patrol's approach or withdrawal. Engineers often are attached to guide a patrol through German minefields and to clear a way through enemy wire or mines. Artillery support is given in the form of harassing fire put down just before the patrol reaches its objective. Sometimes the artillery fires into adjacent sectors to mislead the enemy as to the actual area to be reconnoitered. In other instances, artillery and mortars that have registered during the previous day, shell during the night the area to be reconnoitered. As soon as the barrage is lifted, the patrol advances under cover of machine-gun fire from flanking positions....."

his team were unable to achieve any more, they withdrew and were picked up on the beach by the Navy.

Located between the two batteries to be attacked by the commandos, there were to be two other flank attacks, at Puits and Pourville, where the Germans had additional batteries. The firepower from these positions was sufficient to menace the whole success of the expedition.

The two Canadian regiments chosen for the main assault on Dieppe itself were the Essex Scottish, who were to land on the beach to the east of the Esplanade, and the Royal Hamilton Light Infantry, who were to tackle the west end. The Puits attack was in the hands of the Royal Regiment of Canada, and the South Saskatchewan Regiment was to storm Pourville. In reserve were the Fusiliers Mont Royal and the Royal Marine Commando. The Queen's Own Cameron Highlanders of Canada were to act as a second wave at Pourville and, passing through the South Saskatchewan Regiment, go on to attack the airfield at St Aubin.

A reconnaissance photograph taken by a British Spitfire flying low over Dieppe, provides valuable information for the forthcoming raid. The Spitfire is flying low enough that individuals can be made out on the streets below.

As we have seen, the left flank attack failed, with the German battery staying in action. On the opposite flank there was a very different story. Lord Lovat's Commando was so far away from No. 3 Commando that they had no inkling of the unfortunate meeting with the German vessels. Fortunately, too, news of the action at Berneval did not reach the Germans manning the Varengeville guns.

Right on time at 4.50am the landing-craft carrying No. 4 Commando grounded on the shingle at the foot of the tall cliffs. Only at the very last moment did a German machine gun open up on the British, but the raiders were out of the boats and under cover of the cliffs before the defenders obtained a good sight of them.

A way now had to be found to the top of the cliffs and it was known that it would almost certainly have to be up one of two tracks. The first of these was found to be solidly packed with barbed-wire but the second had not been properly prepared and the Commandos, using bangalore torpedoes, soon cut a way through.

There was a measure of the luck that was sadly lacking for No. 3 Commando in this comparatively easy ascent. There now was another stroke of luck for No. 4. As they exploded their bangalore torpedoes, four cannon-armoured Hurricanes roared overhead, and in the general confusion, the Germans failed to identify the source of the explosions as coming from the beaches.

The Commandos pushed on, knowing that another party had landed a little to the east, at Vasterival, and were due to open the assault on the six 5.9 inch guns in the German battery. This section, under Major D. Mills-Roberts, had made very good progress and before 6am had opened small arms fire on the German gunners. Before the Germans could counter this attack, the Commandos had set up their mortars and, almost at once, scored a major success. A mortar shell hit the charges stacked alongside the German guns and a blinding flash and a huge explosion marked the end of the guns.

At 6.20am, a Very Light signal indicated the opening of Lord Lovat's assault from the west. His troops had pushed inland for about a mile after landing and now waited for a low-level Spitfire attack on the battery before rushing the position. The Spitfires came right on time and then the Commando men went forward with the bayonet. Two officers leading the charge, which had to be made over two hundred and fifty yards of open ground, were killed. Captain P.A. Porteous, RA, took their place and was one of the first to reach the guns, although he had by then been wounded in both thighs. The German garrison, with the exception of four men taken prisoner, was wiped out. Captain Porteous was subsequently awarded the Victoria Cross.

Pleased to be out of it, British troops are once again back in a friendly port in the aftermath of the Dieppe raid.

Already the victim of a German bomb, this British destroyer had to be scuppered by its own forces to prevent capture. This picture was taken at the instant the torpedo slammed into the ship.

The withdrawal of No. 4 Commando was completed in excellent order. Before leaving, the British dead were laid near the guns they had helped to capture, under the Union Jack flag.

Meanwhile, the inner flank attack on the left, at Puits, had run into very strong opposition. As soon as the Royal Regiment of Canada set foot on shore they were met with withering fire. The naval engagement which had involved No. 3 Commando had caused the Royal Regiment to alter course with the result that they arrived twenty minutes late at Puits. The German were ready for them. The Canadians, led by Lieutenant Colonel D.E. Catto, attacked through a deadly cross-fire and suffered heavy casualties. Even those who reached the sea wall, fifty yards from the water's edge, found no shelter from the well placed and heavily defended German guns. Captain G.A. Browne, who, as Forward Observation Officer, was to have directed the supporting fire from the destroyer 'Garth', described the scene. *"Owing to the heavy and accurate fire of*

HANDBOOK ON GERMAN MILITARY FORCES
EXTRACT NO.4
DEFENCE OF TOWNS

".....the Germans regard towns and villages as excellent strongpoints, particularly if the buildings are of masonry. Towns also are regarded as excellent anti-tank positions because of the considerable infantry-artillery effort necessary to neutralise them.

In defending a town or village, the Germans locate their main line of resistance well within the built-up portion; the edges of the town, which provide easy targets for artillery fire, are believed to be too vulnerable. The main line of resistance is laid out irregularly in order to develop flanking fire, and every effort is made to conceal its location until the last possible moment. Minor strongpoints are maintained forward of the line in order to break up attacks and provide additional flanking fire. Cul-de-sacs are organised and attempts made to trap attacking forces in them for destruction by counterattacking mobile reserves. These reserves are kept in readiness within the town itself, but other reserve forces are held outside the town to prevent hostile flanking manoeuvres.

Both occupied and unoccupied buildings are booby-trapped in organising the defended positions. Entrances to buildings are blocked, and all windows opened so as not to disclose those from which fire is maintained. Rooms are darkened, and passages are cut in the walls between buildings. To avoid detection, the Germans fire from the middle of the rooms, and frequently change their positions, while communication is maintained through cellars and over roofs. Machine guns are sited low, usually in basements, to provide better grazing fire. Chimneys and cornices are used as cover for men on roofs; tiles may be removed to provide loopholes. Searchlights are mounted to illuminate fields of fire; in their absence vehicle headlights may be used as substitutes. When houses collapse, the defence is carried on from cellars, and rubble heaps of destroyed areas are organised into strongpoints.

Tanks are considered to be ineffective within a defended town, although the Germans have used them in static, dug-in positions at cross-roads and squares. As a result of their experiences on the Eastern Front, the Germans believe single tanks are too vulnerable to Molotov cocktails, magnetic mines, and explosive charges. When the Germans themselves use these antitank weapons, they employ them from foxholes dug outside the perimeter of the town. Efforts are made to destroy enemy tanks immobilised by anti-tank action, either within or outside the town, in order to prevent their recovery or use as artillery observation posts and machine-gun nests. Antipersonnel mines are interspersed in antitank minefields because the attacking infantry are considered the chief menace.

Assault guns may provide direct defensive support fire if attacking forces break through and disorganise the German position. To secure the added protection afforded by masonry walls, the Germans may locate assault guns or tanks within buildings and use them against hostile armoured vehicles and infantry. Counter-attacks, supported by assault guns or tanks, will not be withheld until the situation has become desperate; indeed, surprise counter-attacks may be launched at any time.

For the defence of village strongpoints special battle commandants are appointed. The battle commandant is usually the senior officer and the tactical commander of all military forces, emergency units, and civil organisations in his area. He has the disciplinary power of a regimental commander.

In the case of fairly small villages, consolidation of the place itself is usually deemed sufficient. For larger localities an outer defence system is constructed in addition to the inner defences.

The perimeter ring position is the most important part of

These Luftwaffe anti-aircraft troops are comparatively well equipped with a half track, which has been converted into a mobile anti-aircraft role. The shortage of anti-aircraft guns meant that there was never sufficient protection for the German armies on the ground in the Normandy campaign.

the inner defences and consists of one or more continuous trench systems, each with a deep main battle zone. The forward edge often is beyond the outskirts of the village, unless this creates unfavourable conditions for the anti-tank defence, in which case it is within the village itself. Artillery and heavy support weapons are employed as whole units in support of the perimeter ring position, although single guns may be detached for the defence of strongpoints and roads. The nearer the fighting approaches the inner ring, the more likely it will be that the Germans will split up the support weapons units for close cooperation with infantry assault groups.

The outer defence system likewise consists of a number of concentric positions, approximately four to six miles apart, so as to force the enemy artillery to displace to engage each one. For defence of larger towns the Germans organise the outside ring about 121/2 to 181/2 miles beyond the outskirts whenever feasible. Beyond this outside defence ring, about 2,200 yards forward, are the advanced positions, with covering units still further forward on main roads and railways.

Patrols of all types, including motorised and cyclist patrols, give early warning of the enemy's approach and keep him under continuous observation. Non-military outposts, such as police sentries, party officials, and local farmers also are used for these duties.

Sector boundaries for companies and battalions are defined from the outside defence ring to the centre of the town or village. Usually they do not coincide with vital main roads, which always are defended by entire companies or battalions. Every strongpoint, defence block (combined adjacent buildings), and sector has local reserves; mobile reserves, consisting of combat groups comprised of infantry, tanks, assault and self-propelled guns, are employed for counter-attacks of a larger scale.

In addition to regular military units the Germans employ emergency units, organised iron, personnel of Army, Navy, and Air Force in town defence. Besides these regularly organised emergency units, improvised emergency units are formed from stragglers, remnants of formations, and units in process of reorganisation. Utilisation of emergency units is only temporary. Their main tasks, of local nature, are protection of headquarters, supply points, airfields, etc, and garrison service in fortifications....."

German troops at rest in an anti-tank ditch. By comparison with the Allied armies German officers at a fairly junior level were expected to take important tactical decisions on the ground. Infantry were trained and expected to take up the position of the next senior officer in the event of a casualty.

the enemy, the Royal Regiment was changed in five minutes from an assault battalion on the offensive to something less than two companies on the defensive, pinned down by fire from positions they could not discover."

The Royal Regiment tried desperately to achieve some measure of success, and there was a number of desperate actions on the part of individuals and isolated groups. Lieutenant W.G.R. Wedd rushed a German pillbox single-handed and killed all the occupants with well- aimed grenades, but was himself killed in the attack. Eventually, it was decided that what remained of the Royal Regiment should be withdrawn and the Navy went in, in an effort to take off the survivors. They were under heavy fire, and one landing craft received a direct hit, but at least some of her occupants were rescued.

The fact remained, however, that the headland immediately east of Dieppe was never cleared of the Germans, and this undoubtedly had a considerable effect on the landings on the main beaches.

The importance of surprise was once again made clear in the other, inner, flank attack. The South Saskatchewan Regiment, commanded by Lieutenant-Colonel C.C.I. Merritt, arrived at Pourville beach only five minutes after zero hour and went ashore encountering only slight opposition. They at once pushed inland and captured their first objectives. As resistance became fiercer, the Canadians still advanced.

The men from Saskatchewan fought their way through Pourville, only to be held up by heavy mortar and machine gun fire when they reached the bridge over the River Scie. It was then that their Colonel arrived and gave them the inspired leadership for which he won the Victoria Cross. The incident was later vividly described by Wallace Reyburn, the Canadian war correspondent:

"As the men got ready to tackle the bridge again, an officer came walking up the street. It was Colonel Merritt. He stopped and spoke to us, taking his tin hat off and mopping the perspiration off his brow as he did so. 'What's the trouble?' he asked. 'That bridge

is a hot spot, sir. We are trying to get across it.' 'Okay, come with me.' Merritt walked out into the middle of the street again and said, 'Now, men, we're going to get across this bridge. Follow me. Don't bunch up. Spread out. Here we go!' And he strode off to the bridge, erect, calm and determined-looking. He showed no sign of concern at the muck that was flying round him. His tin hat dangled from his wrist. and he twirled it around as he walked. Most of the men got across this time. Merritt himself, before that day was through, was to cross that bridge no fewer than six times. He led other men across, saying as he set off, 'Come on over - there's nothing to it.' Colonel Merritt did not return with the South Saskatchewans, although by a miracle he survived the rain of fire to which he so casually exposed himself. He was on the beach as the last of his men left in the subsequent withdrawal, but then, taking some spare Tommy guns and rifles, went back towards Pourville saying, 'I'm going to get even with these swine for what they have done to my regiment.' He was subsequently reported to be a prisoner of war."

German officers compare notes during an orders or 'O' group meeting. Resourcefulness and initiative were highly prized qualities for German junior officers.

The Queen's Own Cameron Highlanders of Canada used the bridgehead established by the South Saskatchewans to follow up. They came in broad daylight and made rapid progress although their Commanding Officer, Lieutenant-Colonel A.C. Gostling, was killed as he stepped ashore. Before the time for withdrawal arrived, they had pushed two miles inland, inflicting heavy casualties on the Germans as they went.

THE ATTACK ON THE TOWN

The frontal attack on the town of Dieppe itself was preceded by a short, sharp bombardment by naval vessels and a low level attack by cannon-firing Spitfires and Hurricanes. Then the Essex Scottish on the left and the Royal Hamilton Light Infantry on the right went in to the assault together. Despite the intense bombardment, the Canadians came under heavy fire from concealed emplacements on

German troops of the Dieppe garrison parade through the town with full martial ceremony. They are on the way to the funeral service held to mark the Canadian dead at the Dieppe raid.

A naval deckhand surveys the sky for signs of the Luftwaffe. The German airforce was a real threat in 1942, but by the time of the Normandy landings in 1944, this threat had been considerably reduced.

HANDBOOK ON GERMAN MILITARY FORCES
EXTRACT NO.5

CONDUCT OF THE DEFENCE

".....German defence of a position, whether hastily prepared or complete in all details, is conducted on the same principles. Unless they are compelled by manpower and materiel shortages to rely on the strength of their positions, the Germans prefer heavy concentrations of fire and powerful, coordinated counterattacks by mobile reserves of all arms. They apply the principle of selecting a point of main effort (Schwerpunkt) to the defence as well as to the attack. This principle necessarily is applied in reverse order in the defensive, the main effort being made opposite the point where the enemy is making his main attack.

German artillery attempts to disrupt a hostile attack before it reaches the defensive positions. The Germans state that it is invaluable to install observation posts simultaneously in the main line of resistance, in the advanced position, and in the immediate vicinity of the gun position. Thus they try to keep a hostile force constantly under observation and fire even when it achieves a penetration. The artillery regiment commander controls the fire as long as possible, although requests for artillery barrages may be made by unit commanders as low as platoon leaders. Capabilities of German heavy mortars, which like all other support weapons usually are sited on reverse slopes, are exploited, with a present trend toward mortar-fire concentration.

When the enemy succeeds in making a large penetration or breakthrough, the German higher echelon commander decides whether a general counter-attack should be launched to restore the position or whether the main battle position should be re-established farther to the rear. The counter-attack is directed against the hostile flank, where possible, and is prepared thoroughly. Assembly area, time, objective, zone, artillery support and employment of tanks, self-propelled artillery, assault guns, and air units are controlled by one commander.

German anti-aircraft defence, which is unable to give adequate protection everywhere because of Allied air supremacy, is concentrated at important points. The main mission of the light and medium antiaircraft artillery is the protection of roads. Accuracy of Allied air reconnaissance compels the German anti-aircraft artillery to change positions from day to day, the changeover being made during the night. The Germans also enforce a preliminary two-hour fire silence in the new position to try to trap enemy fighter-bombers. Searchlights often are placed parallel to a protected road to prevent enemy aircraft from illuminating the road by flares. This is particularly important since the Germans normally bring forward their relief troops, rations, and ammunition during the night....."

The deadly 88mm anti-aircraft gun..

The Canadian victims of the fighting are lowered into fresh graves with great ceremony. It is interesting to contrast the dignified behaviour which characterised these events in the west with the inhuman actions which were taking place on the Eastern front at the same time.

the two headlands east and west of the beaches. The Casino, which had been turned into a powerful strongpoint by the Germans, was stormed by the Royal Hamiltons, strongly assisted by the Royal Canadian Engineers.

Unable to obey his orders to destroy the main telephone exchange in the Post Office because of intense enemy fire, and left in charge of his platoon through the commander and most of the senior NCOs being out of action, Hickson led the platoon to the Casino. There he blasted his way with explosives through the walls and blew in the steel door of a concrete gun emplacement, killing the gun-crew of five. After the Canadians had cleared the post, they completed the demolition work by blowing up the six-inch naval gun which commanded the beach and the main Dieppe approach, and put a couple of machine-guns out of action.

It was then that the first wave of tanks of the 14th Canadian Army Tank battalion arrived in the special tank landing craft. Royal

One of the thousands of massive wooden stakes topped with teller mines which the Germans set up along the invasion coast.

Canadian Engineers worked with desperate courage to make a way for the tanks over the sea wall, which varied in height from eight to ten feet.

One of the features of the Dieppe raid was the first deployment of a new British tank known as the Churchill. These early tanks had specially adapted exhaust outlets to allow them to operate in water up to six feet in depth. Despite the deployment of twenty nine of these, the very latest machines to reach the army, their attack on Dieppe was nothing short of a disaster.

Confronted by a series of concrete anti-tank barricades and an extensive system of anti-tank ditches, the new tanks failed to clear their way off the beach and into the town. Casualties were high and the entry of the Churchill was not an auspicious success. Its baptism of fire suggested that the task ahead might yet prove too great for this ponderous infantry support tank.

Despite the best efforts of the RAF, who fought a vicious duel with the Luftwaffe in the skies above Dieppe, there was little that they could do to influence events on the ground. The failure of the Churchills to clear the concrete defences which the Germans had erected to bar the roads leading into the town, left the infantry without effective tank support; so the Canadian infantry who had reached the shore could make little headway. Nonetheless, the Canadians fought hard, and despite the fact that the tanks could not get off the beach, they actually managed to establish a foothold in the town. But as the superior German forces gained the upper hand, large numbers of exhausted prisoners were gathered together to parade for the cameras, and the German newsreels had an unexpected field day.

The famous images of the knocked-out Churchill tanks proved to be a great propaganda coup for the Germans, who were presented with brand new examples of the latest British technology for study, evaluation and as trophies of war.

Despite the unhappy scenes of defeat, the Dieppe raid did provide a great deal of valuable experience for the Allies, which would be put to use in the D-Day landings two years later. Against all expectations, the Churchills would be back and they would play an essential role in the crucial events of June 1944.

Of the tanks which went to attack the defences on the western headland, the few which turned into the town found themselves shut in by very heavy tank blocks. One of the Churchills smashed clean through a house, only to run into fresh anti-tank guns. About this time the Fusiliers Mont Royal, the floating reserve, were sent in to reinforce the Essex Scottish, but fared no better against the concentrated fire the Germans could still bring to bear on the beaches, particularly as the eastern headland still remained unsubdued. Major General Roberts then decided to send in the Royal Marine Commando.

Few of the Marines actually got ashore, because as soon as they cleared a smoke screen, which had been put down to cover their approach, they came under a tremendous concentration of fire. Lieutenant-Colonel J.P. Phillips, realising that it was useless for

Back once again on British soil, survivors of the raid proudly display the flag which flew briefly above the German guns in Dieppe.

The Allied campaign in Normandy owed much of its success to the incredible level of secrecy which surrounded the operation. The planners were painfully aware of the dangers of a single slip. Propaganda posters were used to great effect to reinforce the need for secrecy among the Allied soldiery. It certainly seems to have worked, as the Germans had no real idea of either the time or the place of the Normandy landings.

them to go on, put on a pair of white gloves and waved to the boats to turn back. He saved the lives of many men but he himself fell mortally wounded.

Meanwhile, units on shore continued to fight on, inflicting heavy casualties on the Germans, until the withdrawal signal was given. The difficulties they faced are later expressed in the official Canadian report on Dieppe: *"Withdrawal following a raid of this sort is always a most difficult and dangerous operation; and in this instance it was especially so as the enemy had succeeded in bringing into action a number of mobile batteries, mortars and additional infantry. Although this enabled him to organise very heavy fire on both the beaches and sea approaches, the ships and craft lying off Dieppe, in spite of excellent fighter cover, were suffering sporadic attacks by dive-bombers. The Navy most gallantly went into the beaches again and again to take off the troops. Officers and other ranks of the military force ashore performed many acts of gallantry in carrying wounded men to the landing craft. During this phase, destroyers closed in on the beaches almost to the point of grounding, in order to support the re-embarkation by fire and to pick up survivors.*

Tribute should here be paid to the heroic work of the doctors and medical orderlies who accompanied the Dieppe forces. They went right in with the fighting battalions and undoubtedly saved many lives by the prompt attention they were able to give while under fire. It was disclosed subsequently that of six hundred Canadians admitted to hospital on return to England, the mortality was only two and a half per cent. Sulphonamides, the new drug series, were extensively used in treating the wounded on the way home and in hospital later, and results were excellent.

Throughout the day, the Royal Navy assisted the land operations by heavy bombardment of enemy shore positions and successfully covered the landings and embarkations. Despite formidable artillery and air opposition, British naval losses, apart from a fairly large number of landing craft (of which, the enemy claimed, three to four hundred were used), consisted only of the Hunt class destroyer 'Berkeley' (904 tons), which was so badly damaged that it had to be sunk by British forces, the majority of the crew being saved."

THE FIGHT IN THE AIR

The last chapter of the tale of Dieppe concerns the air battle which raged over the town practically throughout the land operations. The Germans, alarmed at the strength of the landings, rushed in reserves of aircraft exactly as the RAF had hoped. As a result there developed one of the greatest dogfights of the war. RAF aircraft were sent on more than two thousand sorties. Apart from innumerable dogfights with the Luftwaffe, the planes shot up ground positions, bombed near-by aerodromes, put down smoke screens and covered both the attack and withdrawal. At the end of the day the RAF had lost one hundred and six planes. Luftwaffe losses were significantly lower at forty eight aircraft, nonetheless the costly results of this air action were sufficient to cause the Luftwaffe to make large-scale alterations in their air dispositions immediately after the raid. Rather disguisingly the Prime Minister referred to it as, *"an extremely satisfactory air battle which Fighter Command wish they could repeat every week."*

The far-reaching benefits that accrued to the planning for Overlord as a result of the outstanding bravery of the men who went to Dieppe are easily understandable, but they were purchased at a very high price. Although only one hundred and seventy Canadians were actually killed, out of a force of five thousand, a further 3,260 were wounded or taken prisoner. Nonetheless, they had rendered a lasting service to the Allied cause and even the Germans were forced to join in the praise of their courage. The German controlled Paris radio untypically passed favourable comment, *"The first thing that emerges from the fighting is the stubbornness of these soldiers. One has the impression that these men clung to the soil and fought*

Field Marshal Sir John Greer Dill, Chief of the British Joint Staff Mission to the USA from December 25th 1941 until November 4th 1944.

to the last cartridge and that they were endowed with magnificent courage."

The question that has been most frequently asked since the day when a startled England, and perhaps an even more startled Germany, first heard the news that British Empire troops were fighting on French soil, is, "Was it worth it?" The reply is probably, "Yes." In a sense, Dieppe was the key to the Allied landings in North Africa, Sicily, Salerno, and, of course, Normandy. Although it was a high price that the Canadians troops had to pay when they set foot in France, the final dividend was out of all proportion to that great sacrifice.

THE LESSONS OF DIEPPE

Even as they assessed the results of the operation, the Canadians acknowledged the importance of the raid in an official report issued a month after the attack: *"The United Nations have an agreed offensive policy. In the preparation and development of such a policy, the acquisition of the fullest possible information concerning the enemy's strength and dispositions, and every other element in the situation affecting the conduct of operations against him, is a matter of the most fundamental importance.*

Such information is available from many sources, but it is frequently the case that facts essential to the successful prosecution of offensive operations can only be gained by fighting for them. The Dieppe operation must be regarded in this light. It was considered most important that our forces should have an opportunity for practical experience in the landing, on an enemy-occupied coast, of a large military force, and in particular in the problems arising of the employment in such a force of heavy armoured fighting vehicles."

It was not just the Allies who had learned the lessons of Dieppe. The German High Command also realised that their defences could be improved. In particular, their sea defences needed to be much more effective against the amphibious landing. A careful study of the results of the battle at Dieppe proved the value of both concrete obstacles and anti-tank ditches. In addition, thousands of obstacles were placed beneath the high water mark, which were designed to make it very difficult for the infantry and armour to reach the shore. To complete the task of preparing the Atlantic Wall, Hitler chose Field Marshal Erwin Rommel. He was appointed in January 1944.

- C H A P T E R   2 -
PREPARING FOR 'OVERLORD'

The Dieppe raid gave Churchill, in particular, a much more realistic idea of the difficulties of mounting an operation like Overlord. Although it created considerable strains within the Anglo-American alliance, with the Americans in particular pressing for a more aggressive approach, it was nonetheless agreed at the Casablanca conference of January 1943, that the invasion should not be launched before May 1st 1944.

In the meantime, Churchill prevailed in his long term ambition of mounting an invasion of Italy through Sicily to attack the 'soft underbelly' of Europe. Although this campaign is still hotly debated even today among historians, those actions too, cannot be under-estimated in terms of the lessons that were learned for D-Day.

Sir James Grigg, secretary of state for war, was later to underline the importance in his speech to the House of Commons on March 13th 1945: *"Normally it is not good policy to put a formation into the field unless there is a clear prospect of being able to provide enough reinforcements to keep it up to strength for as long as the operations are likely to last. But the campaign which was to start in the summer of 1944 held the chance of complete and final victory. We therefore decided to throw everything we could into the battle.*

During this period of preparation we mounted and sustained offensives in North Africa and, after the destruction of the enemy there, we invaded Sicily in July of 1943 and Italy two months later. These operations provided many lessons for the new venture and many new devices were specially produced for it. Whether the entire effort of the Allies should have been better preserved for the main invasion in France must remain a matter of conjecture. Nevertheless, the campaign in Italy did succeed in tying down twenty-three German divisions which could otherwise have faced the Allies in Normandy."

In preparation for D-Day, throughout 1942 the RAF had been taking high altitude photographs of the enemy coasts of northern France. By 1943 the emphasis had switched to more detailed, low level surveys of the defences of Fortress Europe. In addition, French resistance sources were called upon to play their part in supplying information on the German forces.

There was also a more unorthodox request, which was made to the public through the BBC, for holiday snaps or postcards of any part of the world. The response was overwhelming and within twenty-four hours the BBC had been inundated with postcards and over ten million pictures were eventually collected. Fifty American service women had to be flown over especially to sort through the postcards. In addition, the Allies began to prepare massive and accurately detailed maps of the areas of France which could potentially be used for the invasion.

Somewhere in southern England, these Royal Marines practice for landing operations on enemy-held territory.

49

The special team, which was based at Oxford University, and led by Royal Marine Colonel Sam Bassett, known as the Interservice Topographical Unit, had the job of collating the information to choose the ideal landing site and they certainly did that job with great skill.

When it came to the choice of the actual invasion beaches, the number of locations was limited by the availability of fighter cover which could be provided from England. The clear choice, of course, was in the Pas de Calais area, which was only twenty-two miles across the Channel from Dover. This, therefore, provided the shortest sea crossing with the army at its most vulnerable, when embarked upon the ships. This was the obvious choice. It was also obvious, however, that this conclusion had similarly been drawn by the Germans, and it was at this point that the very heaviest defences of Fortress Europe were concentrated.

With the lessons of Dieppe still fresh in mind, an attack on Holland was also ruled out because of the difficulties of ensuring the capture of a port, and the strength of the German defences.

'Airborne' training, 2nd October 1942, Netheravon. In 1944, the airborne troops took over the flank protection task undertaken by the Commandos in the Dieppe raid.

HANDBOOK ON GERMAN MILITARY FORCES
EXTRACT NO.6
OBSERVATION POSTS

".....the Germans have constructed special works of reinforced concrete as coast artillery observation and command posts. A typical observation post, Type 636 (for Army Coast Artillery), is shown in Figure 1. Separate rooms are provided for observation, plotting, radar, officers' quarters, and enlisted men's quarters. A Giant Wurzburg radio direction finder is mounted in the emplacement on the roof. For close defence there are two machine-gun loopholes covering the rear entrance: one in the exterior wall, and one in the interior wall at the foot of the stairs. There are quarters for two officers and nine enlisted men, but since this does not accommodate all the personnel on duty at the observation post, a personnel shelter for one section is built nearby.

Field artillery observation posts in a permanent defence line are similar to personnel shelters, with the addition of a steel cupola for the observer.

OBSTACLES
The German tactical use of obstacles differs from the U.S. Army in that they install them within the main battle positions. Obstacles are covered by fire from concrete pillboxes and open emplacements. The Germans employ both fixed and movable permanent obstacles, constructed for the most part of steel, concrete, or both. The most common types are described below.

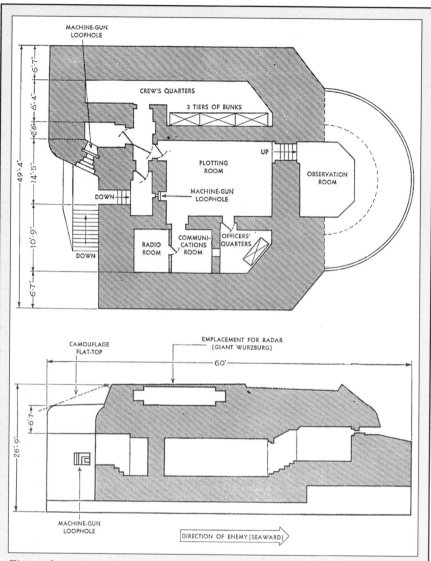

MACHINE-GUN
LOOPHOLE

CREW'S QUARTERS

3 TIERS OF BUNKS

UP

PLOTTING
ROOM

OBSERVATION
ROOM

DOWN

MACHINE-GUN
LOOPHOLE

RADIO
ROOM

COMMUNI-
CATIONS
ROOM

OFFICERS'
QUARTERS

DOWN

49'-4"

6'-7"

8'-4"

2'-6"

14'-5"

10'-9"

6'-7"

CAMOUFLAGE
FLAT-TOP

EMPLACEMENT FOR RADAR
(GIANT WURZBURG)

60'

26'-9"

6'-7"

MACHINE-GUN
LOOPHOLE

DIRECTION OF ENEMY (SEAWARD)

Figure 1

ANTI-TANK OBSTACLES

• Dragon's teeth. A prominent feature of the Westwall
is the anti-tank obstacle called by the Germans 'dragon's
teeth'. These are truncated pyramids of reinforced concrete,
arranged in irregular rows of four or five. The height of the

teeth varies successively from two and a half feet in the first row on the enemy side to five feet in the rear row, so that a tank is made to belly on the obstacle. The teeth are cast in a concrete foundation running from front to rear, and sometimes also along each row, to prevent the teeth from being toppled over.

Dragon's teeth are usually sited in long continuous lines, broken only where roads pass through the line of obstacles and where the terrain is considered unsuitable for tank activity.

• Elements C. The Germans adopted the Belgian de Cointet anti-tank obstacle, more often called 'Elements C', which is illustrated in Figure 2. Here a number of units have been fastened together to form a continuous anti-tank wall, but since the units have rollers in the front and rear, the Germans also use them singly as movable blocks.

Figure 2

• Curved-rail obstacle. Similar to the 'Elements C' is the curve-rail anti tank obstacle, which the Germans used extensively along the Westwall. The curved rail, which slopes upward to a steep angle at the rear, faces the enemy, so that tanks attempting to climb over the obstacle tip-over backward. It usually is made in sections six feet high, three feet wide, and ten feet long.

ROAD BLOCKS
• Steel bars. A road passing through a barrier may be closed by horizontal steel bars arranged successively higher in reinforced concrete slots or by steel rails set upright into the road.
• Tetrahedra. The Germans also block roads with tetrahedra, which consist of steel frames or solid concrete blocks with four faces. The height of a tetrahedron varies from two and a half to four and a half feet, and its purpose is to belly a tank.

BARBED-WIRE OBSTACLES
• A German double-apron fence is illustrated in Figure 3. The fence is 4 to 5 feet high. Knife rests, or chevaux de frise, strung with barbed wire, can be seen to the right of the fence where the road passes through the obstacles. The Germans call knife rests "Spanish riders" and use them as road blocks. German knife rests are about 4 feet high and have angle-iron or timber frames. Concertina wire (S-Rolle) often is used by the Germans either in single, double, or triple coils. Sometimes it is wired to concrete posts, fixed on top of walls, and interwoven with double-apron fences or between concrete dragon's teeth. The Germans also use an obstacle consisting of trip wires (Stolperdraht) arranged

about 30 feet in depth. The wire is stretched from 4 to 8 inches above the ground on irregular rows of wooden pickets. The interval between pickets in rows is 10 to 13 feet and between rows 7 to 10 feet...."

Figure 3

NORMANDY CHOSEN

The final choice then fell upon the remaining option, which was the Normandy coast. It was far enough from the obvious route to have adecoy effect on the Germans thinking, but at the same time it was still well within fighter range and was considerably less well defended than the Pas de Calais. Additionally, if Cherbourg could be captured early on, it would provide an invaluable port for bringing in the supplies which would be required for the massive assemblage of men which would be necessary for the campaign in Europe.

In the event that Cherbourg could not be captured, another

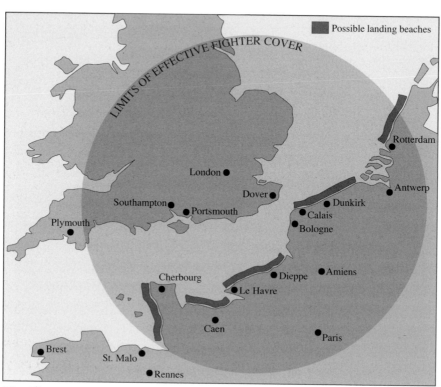

The Dieppe experience had ruled out the option of a direct assault against a heavily defended port. A number of beaches, ranging from Holland to Normandy, presented possibilities for an Allied landing.

enterprise was undertaken, the creation of two artificial harbours, upon which the success of the whole operation could potentially have depended. As the Dieppe raid had shown, an assault against an established enemy port was certain to meet powerful opposition. An assault over open beaches, much less strongly defended, offered by far the best hope of quickly getting a large force ashore. But this was but half the problem. Once ashore, the Army had to be reinforced more rapidly than the Germans. To rely on the quick capture of an established port was to court disaster. The only answer was an assault over open beaches, accompanied by the creation of ports for rapid unloading and reinforcement. In a speech to the House of Commons, Secretary of State for War, Sir James Grigg, recalled other difficulties.

"The conception, like all great conceptions once made, seemed simple. Its fulfilment was an immense task. It required the preparation and sinking of sixty old ships, which provided breakwaters for both the British and American forces by the fourth day of the assault. In addition, two full scale ports, the 'Mulberries', were constructed from six- thousand-ton concrete caissons towed across the Channel. The British port alone used four-and-a-quarter miles of these caissons, weighing approximately 550,000 tons. On the twelfth day of the assault, sixteen hundred tons were discharged at this port, and by the thirty-fourth day an average of six thousand tons a day was discharged."

THE SUPREME COMMAND

Having chosen the landing beaches, it was now time to appoint the supreme command to the Allied Forces which would be gathered together to make the invasions.

Naturally, with the Americans contributing the bulk of the men and equipment, Churchill and Roosevelt quickly agreed that the supreme commander should be an American. There was some debate before Roosevelt made the choice of Eisenhower, who had skilfully planned the 'Operation Torch' landings in North Africa, and who was now in full command of the Allied forces fighting in Italy and the Mediterranean.

As soon as he was appointed to Supreme Command, Eisenhower set up his headquarters at Bushey Park in London's western suburbs and gathered together the very best of the Allied commanders that he could find. Air Chief Marshal Sir Arthur Tedder, was the Deputy Supreme Commander. Air Chief Marshal Sir Trafford Leigh-Mallory, was given command of Allied air forces and Admiral Sir Bertram Ramsey was in charge of the sea forces for the invasion. On land, command fell to General Sir Bernard Montgomery who was to command the forces on the ground. Lieutenant General

Omar Bradley and Lieutenant General Miles Dempsey were named commanders of the main invasion forces, the US First and British Second armies. Eisenhower's long standing Chief of Staff, Major General Walter Beddell Smith, continued his long relationship with Eisenhower. Inevitably, the colourful figure of Montgomery attracted a disproportionate level of interest.

There was some controversy almost from the start of the operation. The initial plan had originally envisaged a three division operation. For Montgomery, it soon became obvious that this would need to be revised to five divisions to guarantee success on D-Day, a development which was clearly recalled by his son over fifty years later.

"When my father was asked to command Operation Overload his first move was to talk to Eisenhower in North Africa and then go to Churchill and explain that the original plan to have a three division

As a result of the thorough planning for Overlord, even the capture of German weather forecasting stations was not overlooked.

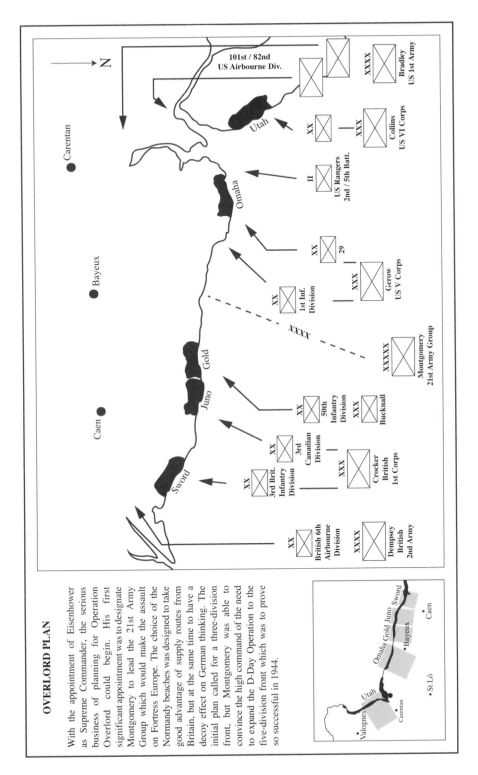

OVERLORD PLAN

With the appointment of Eisenhower as Supreme Commander, the serious business of planning for Operation Overlord could begin. His first significant appointment was to designate Montgomery to lead the 21st Army Group which would make the assault on Fortress Europe. The choice of the Normandy beaches was designed to take good advantage of supply routes from Britain, but at the same time to have a decoy effect on German thinking. The initial plan called for a three-division front, but Montgomery was able to convince the high command of the need to expand the D-Day Operation to the five-division front which was to prove so successful in 1944.

front would not work and it needed to be expanded to a five division plan. Indeed this was the plan that he launched when he got back to England at the beginning of January 1944."

Years after the Battle of Normandy, and even after his own death, Field Marshal Montgomery remains a controversial figure. If he were alive today, that would no doubt have delighted him. Montgomery enjoyed creating controversy, he considered himself as a very important person indeed and, furthermore, as one of the world's great generals of history. With his lively wit he would no doubt have been amused that so long after the events of June 6th, 1944, these arguments still rage.

Montgomery was an extremely capable general, but perhaps not quite as infallible as he suggested he was. Inevitably this was to show in the conduct of the coming battle for Normandy. With hindsight, Montgomery would insist that in Normandy, as for a number of his other battles, he never made a mistake. He stated that the battle began with his drawing up what he called his 'Master Plan' and that there was never any need to deviate from that Master Plan for the course of the campaign. At the end of his life he would suggest, perhaps rather mischievously, that this was exactly what happened. There is no doubt that had the Battle of Normandy been lost, Montgomery would have been blamed very heavily for losing it, and for that reason, he is entitled to enjoy the credit for winning it, as his son was later to recall.

"The main objective of the plan was, in fact, to secure an early bridgehead on this five division front, being three British and Canadian and two American divisions, and having secured the bridge head, the objective of the exercise was to stage a holding operation on the left flank, i.e. around Caen, so as to draw all the German forces there and once the bridgehead had been opened up on the western flank, where the Americans were, to bring in much more numerically superior American forces, in order to have them operate the break out. This was, in fact, by and large, what happened.......

The German forces had had a great deal of battle experience and fought very professionally on both fronts for a very long time. So indeed had the British. An interesting aspect of this is that the American forces, who played such a vital part, of course, had much less battle experience, which I always feel is probably one of the reasons why my father assigned them the break-out role on the west, rather than the holding role down on the eastern front, in the initial stages of the operation.

One of my father's great military maxims was that you had to have co-ordinated forces. Ever since his time in the desert he had always tried to work very closely with the airforce in support of what was happening on the ground and at the time of D-Day the Allied

Towards the end of December 1943, and during January 1944, the names of the men who were to lead the Allied forces in re-opening a Western Front were announced. This photograph, taken in January 1944, shows seated, left to right: Air Chief Marshal Sir Arthur Tedder, Deputy Supreme Commander; General Dwight David Eisenhower, Supreme Commander, Allied Expeditionary Force; General Sir Bernard Law Montgomery, Commander-in-Chief, British Group of Armies; standing, left to right, Lieutenant-General Omar Bradley, Commander-in-Chief, American Group of Armies; Admiral Sir Bertram Ramsay, Allied Naval Commander-in-Chief; Air Chief Marshal Sir Trafford Leigh-Mallory, Allied Air Commander-in-Chief; Lieutenant-General Walter Bedell Smith, US Army.

HANDBOOK ON GERMAN MILITARY FORCES
EXTRACT NO.7
LAYING OF MINEFIELDS

".....to assure the greatest possible effect, minefields normally are laid out in definite patterns. The Germans make an exception to this practice, however, in sectors where they do not intend to undertake offensive actions. There they disperse the mines irregularly in the areas between defensive positions.

The main belts of a major anti-tank minefield laid in uniform pattern normally consist of anti-tank mines with a sprinkling of anti-personnel mines in the forward edge of the field. Both types may be fitted with anti-lifting devices, and some of the anti-personnel mines have trip wires attached. In some instances, these mines are placed in the intervals between the diagonal wires of a double-apron fence, with trip wires fastened to the diagonals.

A number of anti-tank mines are laid in the forward edge of anti-personnel minefields to prevent armoured

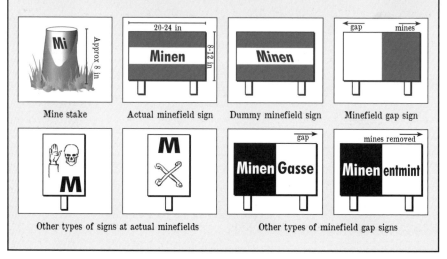

| Mine stake | Actual minefield sign | Dummy minefield sign | Minefield gap sign |

Other types of signs at actual minefields   Other types of minefield gap signs

vehicles from detonating the main belt of anti-personnel mines. The forward edges of minefields of all types often are sown with explosive charges placed in wooden boxes fitted with pressure fuses. These act as both anti-tank and anti-personnel mines, and discourage the use of detectors to locate the mines.

Forward of most regular fields, and particularly in front of lanes, mines may be found widely spaced or scattered at random in unmarked groups. Mines are also laid in spaces running out at right angles from the forward edge of the minefield to damage vehicles moving along the field in search of lanes.

Mine lanes are left open for patrols, and passage lanes for assault troops. For permanent patrols new lanes are made from time to time, and the old ones closed. A mine-free safety strip is provided on the Germans' side.

The Germans emphasise that minefields must be covered by fire, although during a hasty withdrawal they often do not follow this principle. It is common for a regular minefield to have a listening post with two men at the rearward edge; about 70 or 80 yards farther to the rear there usually is a covering party of four or five men armed with one or two light machine guns.

When the Germans are in hasty withdrawal, they usually lay a large number of small nuisance minefields. These fields contain many different types of mines, which often are unmarked and show every evidence of hurried laying. The consequent lack of pattern uniformity makes their detection and clearance a laborious and dangerous task. Though no consistency is noted in layout and types of mines used in such fields, the Germans show certain preferences in their choice of sites for them.

Type of Mine	How Laid	Interval between Mines	Number of Rows	Density per 1 Metre of Front
T-Mine 35	Buried	4m (44 yards)	8	2
			12	3
			16	4
T-Mine 42 T-Mine 43	Laid on Surface	4m (44 yards)	8	2
			12	3
			16	4
	Buried	2m (2.2 yards)	4	2
			6	3
			8	4
R-Mine 43	Buried or Laid on Surface	about 4m (44 yards)	2	0.5
			4	1
S-Mine 35	Buried	4m (44 yards)	4	1
			8	2
			12	3
		2m (2.2 yards)	2	1
			4	2
			6	3
Schu Mine 42	Buried	1m (1.1 yards)	1	1
			2	2
			3	3
		0.5m (0.55 yards)	1	2
			2	4

LOCATION

In general, mines are laid either close to, or on, roads; on airfields and railways and along telegraph routes. Surfaced portions of roads usually are avoided by the hasty mine layer, but khaki-painted T-Mines sometimes are placed on the surface at dips in the road, in the hope that drivers will be unable to check their vehicles in time to avoid them. The Germans also place mines along the shoulders of the road opposite narrow places where drivers have to detour to pass, and at the entrances to defiles where they have to pull off the road to wait for vehicles moving in the opposite direction. Other places usually sown with anti-tank mines are turnouts, sharp bends, the unsurfaced islands sometimes found at crossroads, berms, and well worn wheel ruts.

CONCEALMENT

The Germans, with great ingenuity, attempt to make their mines difficult to detect. They bury them as much as 24 inches below the surface where they explode only after passage of a number of vehicles has compacted the earth cover sufficiently to operate the fuse. They put explosives in wooden boxes to prevent the effective operation of ordinary mine detectors, and mark tire prints in the earth on top of the mine...."

airforces played a very big role; first of all in bombing the supply routes, the railways, junctions etc. Aided and assisted, of course, by the resistance on the ground entrenched, and so the Allied airforces played a vital role and, of course, also in transporting the airborne forces, because there was a massive parachute deployment which took place at the same time."

OPERATION ANVIL

One of the few sources of disagreement in the Allied camp, concerned the invasion of Southern France which was scheduled to commence just weeks after the main landings in Normandy.

The incredible logistical task of supplying the armies and fleets involved in the D-Day landings is neatly demonstrated by the bakehouse on board this British warship. This is just a portion of one day's rations for one ship among thousands.

Originally known as 'Operation Anvil', this operation meant that amphibious craft and very large ground forces had to be withdrawn from the Italian theatre; and, consequently, Churchill's under-performing project in Italy was further down-graded in terms of priority.

Churchill, throughout his career, was a great advocate for diverse actions taking place on numerous fronts, in particular amphibious actions. He had been the champion of Gallipoli during the Great War and it was he who had personally championed the idea of attacking what he described as the *"soft underbelly of Europe"* through Italy. So it is not surprising that there were such great rumblings from him at the prospect of the Italian theatre being depleted in favour of new landings in southern France. Nonetheless, Churchill was ultimately forced to relent, although he insisted that the code name should be changed from 'Operation Anvil' to 'Operation Dragoon', to demonstrate that he had been 'dragooned' into agreement. In Normandy too there was still an enormous pressure on the available landing craft, with a consequence that Operation Overlord was further pushed back from a planned May start date, into June 1944.

PLANNING FOR OVERLORD

The Allied plan for the Battle of Normandy which was drawn up in the early months of 1944, after preliminary work which had lasted almost a year beforehand, was exceptionally sound and exceptionally safe. This was a battle which absolutely had to succeed. As nothing is ever certain in warfare, the Allies planned with a great deal of caution, preparing, for a myriad of extra contingencies, most of which mercifully failed to materialise but which had to be catered for in any event. Fortunately, the Allies in Normandy enjoyed better luck than the unfortunate attackers of Dieppe. Nevertheless at times when things did go badly, the extra security and planning was invaluable; it was to prove to be one of the great unsung factors behind the victory.

Sir James Grigg, Secretary of State for War, later underlined some of the planning which had been undertaken.

General Sir Bernard Montgomery in discussion with Air Chief Marshal Sir Trafford Leigh-Mallory.

"Of the entirely new devices the most notable, perhaps, was the prefabricated harbour the 'Mulberry.' But there were countless other military possibilities to be accounted for. A set of spare lock gates for the Caen canal were constructed and made ready to be floated over complete in case the Germans destroyed the existing gates. And again spare parts and assemblies for the repair of vehicles damaged in the early days were packed in special cases such that the required part could be found in the dark and issued without delay. Two million twenty-four hour rations, specially packed in waterproof covers, were issued in the period immediately after landing, together with three million self-heating tins of soup and cocoa. Three and a half million cases of compo rations, sixty million gallons of tinned petrol and sixteen thousand tons of coal packed in five hundred thousand special rot-proof bags were got ready for early shipment. Twenty thousand feet of railway bridging and twenty-five thousand tons of steel trestling were prepared to reconstruct our supply lines as we advanced. In the last fourteen*

A Spitfire safely crossing the English coast on its return from a reconnaissance mission over German occupied Europe.

days alone, Ordnance Depots issued one hundred and fifty thousand miles of telephone cable and eleven million yards of minefield tracing-tape.

Then began the movement to marshalling areas. The marshalling camps, which had been constructed near to all the ports of embarkation, were designed for two main purposes. First, they enabled the movements staffs to sort out each unit into appropriate craft loads, and secondly, they served as hotels where troops arriving and departing at all hours of the day and night could be fed, bathed, accommodated and supplied with all their last-minute needs. It was in these camps, too, that the final stages of the waterproofing of vehicles were carried out. In all one hundred and fifty thousand were waterproofed, and despite the fact that many of them went ashore through five feet of water in heavy seas, less than two in every thousand were drowned off the beaches."

THE ALLIED AIR

Although the planning again generally went smoothly, there was some controversy, in particular over the use of the Allied bomber forces. Indeed, the arguments took on such a fierce dimension that Eisenhower was on the brink of offering his resignation on the thorny issue of just how the Allied bomber forces should be deployed.

Eisenhower demanded full use of the Allied bomber forces to carry out a campaign of interdiction to attack railway lines, bridges and routes which would supply the German armies in Normandy. The leaders of both the British and the American bomber forces, however, were adamant that these scarce resources should be used to continue the air war against the German cities. Air Chief Marshal Sir Arthur Harris, in particular, was highly critical of Eisenhower's plan. It should be noted that he was supported by US Lieutenant General Carl Spaatz, who was also incensed by the proposal. Harris, in fact, believed that the power of his bomber forces could win the war without even the need for the land campaign and Spaatz was very keen to concentrate his bombers on oil targets. Finally, it required the personal intervention of both Roosevelt and Churchill to sort out the impasse and the priority bombing of targets related to the invasion actually started on April 1st 1944. By then, all sides had been reconciled and the cohesiveness of the Allied forces was already established.

After the war some very interesting statistics emerged, which appear to suggest that Spaatz may have been correct in his strategy of bombing targets in Germany. In particular he had seen Germany's synthetic oil plants as one of the principal targets, and even the limited bombing programme which he was able to continue in May of 1944 produced some spectacular results. Although only something like eleven per cent of his bombing force was available for these duties and approximately twenty per cent in July and August, he was able to bring about a fall in German synthetic oil production, which tumbled from 927,000 tonnes in March to 715,000 tonnes in May before dwindling to 472,000 tonnes in June. This had a particularly disastrous effect on the Luftwaffe, which relied upon supplies of fuel to keep its aircraft flying in the face of overwhelming Allied air superiority.

It is probably stretching the point to suggest, as Spaatz did, that the continuation of this bombing campaign would have been enough to conclude the war against Germany but it is certainly interesting to speculate whether the resistance would have been so prolonged had the oil stranglehold really began to take hold.

Sir Archibald Sinclair, secretary of State for Air commented in 1945:

"In the late spring, the destruction of German communications behind the intended invasion front took first place among our bombing objectives. It was not a task upon which the Allied Air Forces entered lightheartedly, for it involved the destruction of railway facilities, some of which were in thickly populated areas

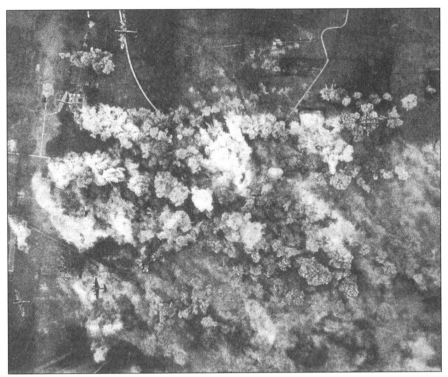

Lancaster bombers attack an SS Panzer Division as it moves up through the village of Villers-Bocage.

of France. Marshalling yards and railway repair facilities were destroyed on a great scale. Twenty-four road and railway bridges over the Seine were selected for bombing; by D-Day all twenty-four had been either demolished or severely damaged. The result was to destroy one of the main assumptions on which the enemy's plan of defence was based. He had naturally assumed that he could reinforce his defensive front by road and rail more quickly than we could reinforce by sea. As things turned out, the weather favoured this calculation and for three critical days it was impossible to land troops or supplies over the beaches. Nevertheless, so thoroughly had the Allied Air Forces done their work and so complete was the mastery of the British and American Tactical Air Forces over the French roads and railways by day, that the Allied armies were able to reinforce much more rapidly than the Germans."

AIR SUPREMACY

As D-Day approached, Allied air supremacy over the Normandy invasion area and then further into France, was of fundamental importance to the success of the campaign in north west Europe. By the late spring of 1944 the Luftwaffe had, to all intents and purposes, been driven from the skies in the Normandy area. The air supremacy possessed by the Allies was to be put to extremely good use during the coming battle of Normandy. Allied bombers could reduce German beach defences and cut German lines of communication, thus paralysing the build up of German forces opposite the amphibious and airborne British and American forces. Tactical air support would also create absolute havoc for any German unit in Normandy foolish enough to try to move in strength by day. In addition, strategic air power was also to be used as a preliminary bombardment before many of the most important Allied offensives in the Normandy campaign. Air supremacy was therefore a vital feature of the Normandy campaign.

THE ALLIED NAVY

The Royal Navy's role on 6th June 1944 and for several months afterwards was to prove absolutely indispensable to the success of Operation Overlord. Approximately eighty per cent of the thousands of vessels that were used, were crewed by British personnel. Even in the American beach sectors, the landing craft were actually crewed mainly by members of the Royal Naval Reserve and the Royal Naval Volunteer Reserve. Their contribution to D-Day is frequently forgotten.

By 6th June 1944, the combined navies of the Allied nations had made the English Channel virtually impenetrable in terms of any significant German naval attacks. Certainly the D-Day area was well sealed off from German attacks with a very few exceptions by

6th June. Nevertheless, on the morning of 6th June 1944, thirty-six German U-Boats sailed from ports in the Brittany peninsula, with the aim of disrupting the Allied invasion attempt. The Allied anti-submarine screens, however, were actually so dense that it would not be until 14th June that any of these U-Boats got anywhere near the invasion beaches; by which point, huge numbers of troops and masses of material had been landed. Even then they were able to achieve only very small attritional losses at high cost to themselves. Sir Archibald Sinclair, in his speech to the House of Commons on March 6th, 1945 also noted the contribution of the Naval forces.

"D-Day for the British and American armies of liberation was June 6 last year, but for the Royal Air Force the campaign had started long before. The weight of our invasion of Northern Europe would have been much reduced if the U-boats had been sinking even a fraction of the number of Allied ships which they were sinking in every month of the year 1943. Gradually, however, the squadrons of

A U-Boat setting out to sea. By 1944 this threat had been all but defeated by the Allies. As soon as the news of the landings was confirmed over thirty U-boats set sail from their bases, but U-Boat losses were considerable and damage to the Allied fleet was minimal.

Coastal Command, working in closest co-operation with the escort groups of the Royal Navy, had obtained an increasing mastery of the German submarines. Bomber Command. too, had contributed largely to this result by bombing the U-boats in their assembly yards and in their pens, and by their arduous, difficult and extremely successful mining operations.

The Germans had boasted that, thanks to the U-boat, no Allied soldier would set foot on the Continent of Europe. Coastal Command and the Royal Navy answered this boast with deeds. Together they swept the seas and kept open those channel lanes on which depended the security of our convoys and the nourishment of our armies.

In the opening stages of the great battle for Normandy, the burden of the fighting lay principally on Coastal Command. In the three weeks before D-Day, Admiral Doenitz was endeavouring to move up his reserves of U-boats from their bases in Norway, to the threatened area of the Channel Coast. From Norway these U-boats began to slink out on their long trek through Northern and Atlantic waters to the Channel. The Commander-in-Chief, Coastal Command Sir Sholto Douglas, had anticipated every move they made. Knowing what they had to expect, the German Command had given their crews a concentrated course of training against air attack. In particular they were equipped with a new 37mm anti-aircraft gun. Their foresight was wise but unavailing, for these reinforcements were attacked and mauled by aircraft of Coastal Command. In the continuous daylight of the northern summer, the battle was joined off the coasts of Norway, the Shetlands and the Faroes and even in the Arctic when the U-boats sought to escape the range of our aircraft. Many were sunk and damaged.

This was the opening bout. The main campaign, fought in the English Channel and its Western approaches, began on D-Day. Previous to that date, single U-boats had penetrated into coastal waters with the aid of Schnorkels. When the invasion came, the Biscay U-boat fleet made their way to the Western approaches

An illustration from the US Army Handbook shows a German soldier wearing the camouflage smock which was first adopted by the SS units as early as 1939. These suits were initially ridiculed by other elements of the army but proved their use in combat. They were particularly well-suited to the terrain encountered in Normandy.

of the Channel on the surface. They were instantly engaged by Coastal Command, and U-boat prisoners have frankly admitted that entering the Channel was a nightmare. During the first four critical days after D-Day, the Command made thirty-eight sightings, which resulted in several destructive attacks.

These successes of Coastal Command, won in unison with the Royal Navy, were decisive; a blow was inflicted on the enemy from which he never recovered."

- CHAPTER 3 -

INSIDE THE THIRD REICH

Hitler's criminal resolve to fight on, "until five minutes past twelve," not only caused the German people incomparably more death and destruction than they need have suffered, it also cost the Allies tens of thousands of lives. When the year 1944 started, there was still a chance that utter lunacy might be avoided. There were still strong forces in existence which considered it possible to prevent the Nazi hierarchy from pursuing its policy to the bitter end.

By far the most important centre of this potential resistance was to be found in the German Army. The relations between the German Army, or rather the old German officers' caste, and the Nazi Party were a matter for political speculation from the beginning of the Hitler regime. There was no wide rift between the two before 1939, and while the war continued its favourable progress.

When Germany was no longer victorious, however, things began to change. Hitler came to distrust the generals and started to force upon them a ruinous strategy, the folly of which became apparent at Stalingrad and Tunis. The generals resented this, and they realised that, from a military point of view, the war was already as good as lost.

They did not all react in the same way. Some, in particular the younger officers, had accepted the Nazi doctrine whole. But others clearly saw what was happening, and during the winter of 1943-44, scores of German generals who were prisoners in Russia, joined the Kremlin-sponsored German Officers' Union, and started to exhort the German people, over the Moscow radio, to overthrow Hitler and end the war.

At least some of the senior officers of the Army in Germany, (who did not feel themselves bound by the ban on listening to enemy broadcasts), were impressed by the voices of Field-Marshal von

Paulus, Generals von Seydlitz, Daniels and others. Most of them had no need to be told by their comrades in Russian prison camps how things stood. Yet the advice to overthrow Hitler was easier to give than to follow. To carry it out needed the most careful political and military preparation.

A significant section of the officer corps were more or less united in the knowledge that Hitler was fast destroying, not only German material resources, but the German people as well; but they had no clear vision of what should be done after successful revolt. Their fundamental motives were also dubious. Comparatively few of them despised Hitler and the Nazi regime as such. Some may have been driven by sincere concern over the fate of their people, but others simply thought in terms of 1918. The war had been lost, and that was unfortunate, but what mattered most was to save, as had been done twenty-six years before, the German military tradition, the General Staff, and with it, the nucleus of a new German Army. By doing so, there still existed the possibility of trying again.

The job of the anti-aircraft crews had eased by the time of D-Day. The German Luftwaffe hardly made an appearance during the Normandy landings and was even scarcer in the subsequent battles.

Rommel and Hitler pictured together early in 1944. After the war, the myth grew that Rommel had been the good German who was hostile to the Nazi cause. In practice, Rommel was a dedicated follower of Hitler and remained very loyal to the Fuhrer until 1944, when he appears finally to have become convinced that it was no longer possible to win the war.

CHARACTERISTICS OF FORTIFICATIONS

".....the basic consider-ations in the design of German fortifications are fire effect, cover, and concealment. Fire effect has first priority; natural concealment is used as much as possible by blending positions with the surrounding terrain. Personnel and supply shelters, in the construction of which fire effect need not be taken into consideration, are completely below ground level, or as low as the water-table level permits. In order to present as small a target as possible to high angle fire and bombing, emplacements, pillboxes, and casemates are built no larger than necessary to permit crews to operate their guns.

CONSTRUCTION

GENERAL

All permanent, fortress-type works and many field works are of concrete reinforced with steel. Some field works, however, are of masonry, brick, or timber. Steel also is used in concrete structures for beams, turrets, cupolas, gun shields, machine-gun loopholes, and doors. These installations are prefabricated and are assigned code or model numbers. The concrete works themselves are designated by type number and are constructed from plans prepared in the Army Ordnance Office.

THICKNESS OF CONCRETE

The usual thickness of concrete walls and roofs is 6 feet 6 inches (2 metres); smaller thicknesses are found as a rule only in the small field works. In casemates the minimum thickness of the walls and roof is 6 feet 6 inches, and generally increases commen-surately with the calibre of the gun.

REINFORCEMENT OF CONCRETE

Most German concrete fortifications are reinforced with steel bars running in three dimensions to form cubes of ten or twelve inch sides. The diameter of the bars, which are hooked at both ends, varies from 3/8 inch to 5/8 inch, the most common size being 1/2 inch.

The roof over the interior compartments in most structures is supported by steel I-beams, encased in the concrete roof. The size of the beams depends on length of the span. Steel plates laid between the I-beams, and resting on the lower flanges, form the ceiling of the structure. These plates prevent the inside of the roof from falling if the structure sustains a direct hit from artillery shells or aerial bombs. In some cases, the roof is supported by reinforced-concrete beams instead of the steel I-beams, apparently to save critical material.

OPEN EMPLACEMENTS

'TOBRUK' TYPE

From experience in the North African campaign, the Germans derived a type of open, circular pit lined with concrete, which they called a "Tobruk". Hitler subsequently ordered Tobruk pits to be used as defence works in the field, and instructions for building them were distributed down to divisions. A Tobruk pit, which consists of a concrete weapon chamber with a neck-like opening at the top, is built entirely underground. The concrete usually is reinforced. Tobruks vary in size, depending on the weapon mounted in them, but the diameter of the neck is kept as small as possible to reduce the risk of direct hits. Instructions to German troops insist that a Tobruk should not have a concrete roof, since this would reveal the position to the enemy. A board of irregular shape, used as a lid, camouflages the circular opening and keeps out rain.

TOBRUK 58C

The most common type of Tobruk is designated 58c by the Germans. It also is called a Ringstand from a rail that runs around the inside of the neck. The rail provides a track for rotating a machine-gun mount, thus giving the gun a 360-degree traverse. This type of Tobruk has an ammunition chamber, which also serves as an underground entrance.

MORTAR EMPLACEMENT

A Tobruk used as a mortar emplacement, such as Type 61a, is larger than a Ringstand and has a concrete base in the centre of the pit for mounting the mortar. This type also is combined with an ammunition magazine.

PANZERSTELLUNG

The German also have used a Tobruk as a base for a tank turret, usually taken from a French Renault 35. Such an installation, called a Panzerstellung, has a turret armed with an anti-tank gun and a machine gun coaxially mounted. The turret is bolted to a circular metal plate, which is rotated by hand on wheels around a track in the top of the pit affording a 360-degree arc of fire....."

THE NAZI LEADERSHIP

No such long term view was taken by the Nazi leaders. They knew, and said openly, that they were not likely to have another chance. For them defeat meant the end, for themselves personally, and, probably, for their movement also, and their idea of a German world conquest. They did not want to acknowledge defeat so long as a 'miracle', such as a split between the Allies, did not seem utterly impossible. The Nazi leaders knew that the chances of bringing about such a 'miracle' by propaganda alone were slender. But a number of new weapons had been for some time in preparation, ranging from long-range missiles to be launched against southern England, through jet planes and a number of 'One-Man-Weapons' to new types of U-boats, and these might tire out Britain to such an extent that she might be prepared to conclude a compromise peace. Finally, the Nazi politicians thought that, should defeat prove unavoidable, the war should be drawn out as long as possible. The destruction thus wrought all over Europe would lead to a chaos in which they would have much more chance to continue a sort of guerrilla war, and so keep Nazism alive as an underground movement. For all these reasons the ruling group, inside which Himmler had become by far the most powerful figure, were resolved to crush any move towards giving in.

ALLIED BOMBING

For four years the Allied Air Force was the major force from the West carrying the war to Germany. From Dunkirk to D-Day they harried and pounded German war industry and transport. Had not the Luftwaffe been out-fought in the air, hammered on its airfields and smashed in its factories, there could have been no invasion of Normandy.

Allied air bombing was on such a colossal scale that Dr Goebbels even had to admit that, *"it can now hardly be borne."* In the week ending February 12th, 16,000 tons of bombs were dropped by the Allied Air Forces. This rose to 23,000 tons the next week, to 41,000 the week after that and in the following week 32,000 tons, with some returns outstanding. This swelling crescendo of destruction was engulfing oil plants, tank factories and the communications of the German armies on every front, as from West, East and South the Allied Armies surged forward into Germany.

A government order, announced on January 4th, empowered the Reich Youth Leader Axmann to, "accelerate the employment of German youth for auxiliary war tasks," (such as the servicing of anti-aircraft batteries), and to, "regulate find direct the employment of German youth for war purposes," these decisions affecting all boys and girls over ten years of age. Classes of schoolboys were sent, under the leadership of young and reliable Nazi teachers, to do war work. Teaching was left for occasional spare hours. One of the main purposes of this and other measures was to break up the unity of families. Nazi rule had always tended towards 'atomisation' of the people, since this made organised resistance much more difficult.

Difficulties with development meant that the ME262 did not prove to be the war-winning innovation which the Luftwaffe needed.

PILLBOXES AND CASEMATES

CONSTRUCTION

".....although the Germans have a number of types of pillboxes and casemates, most infantry and artillery weapons are installed in open rather than closed emplacements. In accordance with German doctrine, pillboxes and casemates are supported by open field works. Pillboxes may have wall and roof thicknesses of as little as 2 feet; indeed, some of the earliest examples built on the Westwall had thicknesses of only 1 foot. This was increased, however, until all pillboxes had at least the standard thickness of 6 feet 6 inches. Casemates, which house guns of large calibre, have at least the standard thickness of 6 feet 6 inches. Pillboxes and casemates usually have a stepped embrasure to prevent bullets from ricocheting into the gun opening. In addition, a steel gun shield may close the opening.

• Local designs. Some pillboxes are found which do not conform to standard types and are apparently of local design. The Germans often construct a pillbox by mounting a steel turret on an open emplacement, and many pillboxes along the French coast were built by mounting a tank turret over a pit in the sea wall.

• Type 685 casemate. Figure 6 illustrates a typical German casemate, Type 685, for the 210-mm or 128-mm anti-aircraft guns. Most casemates are of this simple design, consisting of a gun room with recesses for ammunition, but some may provide quarters for the gun crew. The walls and roof of Type 685 are 11 feet 5 inches (3.5 meters) thick. The embrasure permits a traverse of 60 degrees and an elevation of 45 degrees. A number of similar casemates have embrasures for a traverse of 90 degrees or 120 degrees. Additional protection and camouflage are afforded by banking the sides and by covering the top with a 2 foot 6 inch layer of earth.

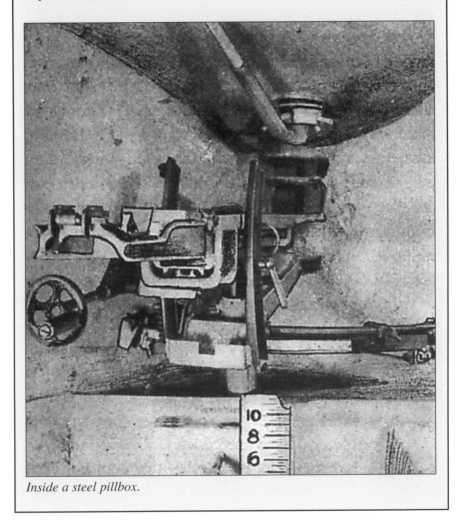

Inside a steel pillbox.

CAMOUFLAGE

To camouflage pillboxes and casemates, earth is banked over the sides and top, the entrance in the rear is covered by a flat-top, and a camouflage net may be hung in front of the embrasure while the gun is not in action. In the case of small pillboxes, branches may be placed over the embrasure. The Germans also conceal pillboxes and casemates by enclosing them in wooden structures resembling ordinary houses. The guns then are fired through false doors or windows, or a section of the wall over the embrasure is made to drop out of the way."

Construction work underway on the section of the Atlantic wall defences in the Pas de Calais area. The Atlantic wall was a massive undertaking, which in reality, could never have been completed in the form envisaged by Rommel and Hitler. Nonetheless, the actual choice of Allied landing beaches was fairly limited, and in the real danger areas, defences were both extensive and substantial.

In January also, all senior generals of the German Army were ordered to Berlin to listen to Goebbels, who gave them a lecture on the situation. That a 'pep talk' of this sort was considered necessary by Goebbels and approved by Himmler, (whom Goebbels had learned to fear and obey), showed that the Party suspected the loyalty of the Army.

SS FAVOURITISM

As the Russian spring campaign swept on, German forces were surrounded and annihilated near Korsun. A tiny proportion of the doomed army was evacuated by air but while none of the units of the regular German Army was saved, significant elements of the SS Viking Division were extricated. This was only one, although perhaps the most spectacular, of many incidents, which increased the impression that the Fuhrer's headquarters regarded units of the SS, the militant Nazi Army, as far more valuable and reliable than most units of the regular Army. This was realised and commented on in the Army, from privates up to senior officers.

In March, three Luftwaffe generals were sentenced to death by court martial, allegedly because of cowardice. They had disobeyed orders during the campaign in the Ukraine. Two were shot at once. The third, a close friend of Goering's, and a man popular with most of the high officers of southern Germany, was saved when Goering intervened for him. He was given the choice of being either shot or degraded to the rank of private. He chose the latter, saying that Germany now needed efficient people in every rank more than ever.

At that time, two symptoms indicated that the rank and file of the Army were growing more and more tired of the war. Firstly, considerably more men in relation to the number of killed and wounded were now being taken prisoner by the Russians. Secondly, a growing number of men deserted while on leave and hid under false names. Their best chance of doing this happened if the city in which they spent their leave was subjected to Allied air attack. They could then disappear, as victims of the air raid. It was not too difficult for them to go into hiding, or to assume another name, as many of the civil registers were destroyed by Allied bombs, and there was a regular black market in false identity papers.

The Nazis could not hope to re-educate the average German senior officer to the point of putting the Party above the Army. But they strengthened those whom they considered reliable, and promoted to important positions younger officers who had not been soaked, like their seniors, in the Army tradition, but whose whole thinking had been imbued by Nazi ideologies. In March 1944, a 'general inspectorate to supervise the education of new leaders at the High Command of the Army', (Generalinspekteur fuer den Fuehrungsoffiziere beim Oberkommando des Heeres), was created.

A more important step, announced on May 20th, was the institution of "National-sozialistische Fuehrungsoffiziere", (National Socialist leadership officers). These were an exact imitation of the Political Commissars who had previously existed within the Red Army, been reintroduced after the outbreak of war, and then, when the Russian High Command realised that it could rely on the loyalty of the Army, converted into regularly commissioned officers. But German propaganda had always insisted that without the terrorist rule of the Political Commissars, the Red Army would never have fought. Now they had to explain the necessity of establishing a similar institution in the German Army.

To counteract civilian anxiety about the growing danger of invasion from the West, German propaganda boasted the impenetrable Atlantic Wall which, it was said, would make a successful Allied landing impossible. It was, in fact, highly desirable that the Allies should make the attempt, as its certain defeat might hasten the end of the war. Later, it was sometimes conceded that the Allies might gain a small foothold somewhere, but that this would give the German Army all the more opportunity of destroying the expeditionary force of the Allies.

In the early part of the war, the Wehrmacht retained a complete cavalry division, but even in 1944 a considerable proportion of the transport and logistical backup was horse drawn.

ROMMEL APPOINTED

In January 1944, Field-Marshal Rommel, who, despite his defeats in Africa, was still the most popular German general, was appointed to supervise the defence of the coastlines of France and the Low Countries. But even Rommel would prove incapable of stemming the tide.

While a western front was now an impending threat, the eastern front was also moving again. The Russians smashed the 'Fatherland Line' along the upper Dnieper, then engulfed its northern and southern flanks, moved deep into central Poland and caused the German Army losses of more than half a million men within a month. Again Hitler's personal strategy prevailed over the advice of his generals; the Baltic countries were not evacuated and an army of more than thirty divisions was thus cut off.

A V2 rocket captured by the Allies while still in the course of production in an underground assembly plant at Nordhausen.

GOEBBELS' PROPAGANDA

There was only one thing about which German propaganda could boast: the launching of hundreds of flying bombs from the Pas de Calais against Britain. The destruction wrought in London and southern England was grossly exaggerated. By fantastic inventions and exaggerations as to the damage done and the 'desperation of the English', Nazi propaganda succeeded for a short time in making at least some part of the German people believe that "German science and new German weapons" could still compensate for Allied superiority in men and material. But those with more insight into the real state of affairs knew better. The commanders of the German Army saw clearly that the much-advertised Vergeltungswaffen, (reprisal weapons), campaign was a military failure. Its start had been delayed by months; it had been hoped that the Allies would feel themselves forced to attack the V-weapon coast, (the Pas-de-Calais), where very strong German forces were waiting behind particularly formidable coastal defences.

But the Allies did not fall into this trap. The German generals had to fight a war on three European fronts, and a 'Fourth Front' - the air front - against which the Luftwaffe, weakened by the concentration of effort upon the development of V-weapons, proved powerless, was steadily obliterating German production and communication centres. The army commanders saw clearly that it was only a question of a short time before Eisenhower's army broke out of Normandy.

- CHAPTER 4 -

THE ALLIED BUILD UP

Since 1942 there had been a huge build up of US men and materials to support the invasion of continental Europe. In 1944 over 950,000 US troops were poised to strike from Britain. In addition they brought with them the entire panoply of modern warfare. Thousands upon thousands of tanks, trucks, artillery pieces and the accompanying logistical support cluttered the south of England. In addition, the British forces were steadily withdrawn from Italy to provide the core of the British Second Army which would take part in the forthcoming operation.

THE BRITISH ARMY

The British army, assembled for the Battle of Normandy, was as successful and as capable as any army has ever been in history. It had its faults and it had its problems and it was perfectly prepared to acknowledge these. It also had a sense of modesty, perhaps too much modesty, but in the spirit of the time it was inclined to praise its enemies rather more than itself, and this has perhaps misled both a number of its Allies at the time and a number of historians ever since. If the British army had been as bad as the German army, then the Battle of Normandy just could not have been fought and won. This trend was also noted by Viscount Montgomery in a television interview concerning his father's role in the campaign:

"One of the problems which historians sometimes have in discussing the Battle of Normandy is that German forces which had seen previous combat experience are nearly always described as 'veteran', whereas British forces that had previous combat experience are more often described as 'burnt-out'. It is true that

some of the German forces were combat experienced, but some, like the 12th SS Panzer, the Hitler Jugend, were going into action for the first time. But that is equally true of British, Canadian and American forces.

Some of the German forces had had a great deal of battle experience and many fought very professionally on both fronts for a very long time. So indeed had the British. The interesting aspect of this is that the American forces, who played such a vital part of course, had much less battle experience, which I always feel is probably one of the reasons why my father assigned them the break-out role rather than the holding role in the initial stages of the operation."

British Churchill tanks being put through their paces in 1942. Although this tank had performed disastrously in the Dieppe raid, it was to prove particularly useful to the 79th Armoured Division during the Normandy campaign.

THE SECURITY WAR

Obviously there were enormous security implications for such a massive build up. One significant advantage for the Allies, however, was the fact that the Luftwaffe had long lost control of the skies. They were busy fighting what was increasingly a losing battle in the skies over Germany, and reconnaissance flights were both few and far between and also very dangerous for the German crews who flew them.

In consequence, Germany found itself starved of precise information as to the actual ports which were to be used, and the size and scale of the build up which would be used against them. It is one of the great triumphs of the build up to Operation Overlord that such a huge build up was covered by such a successful secrecy attempt. There were, of course, a few scares. No operation of such a size and such an undertaking could hope to maintain such complete silence.

British paratroops are seen on board their aircraft preparing for a drop into action. The mixture of emotions can be seen in their tense faces.

Churchill arrives in Normandy on June 12th 1944 -the sixth day after the first landings.

DISASTER IN THE CHANNEL

The Allied planners worked on the assumption that if the Germans received even forty-eight hours warning of the location of the assault area, the chances of successes were very small.

One of the chief scares came on the night and early morning of April 27th and 28th when convoy T4, a US training operation, was attacked by seven German E-Boats which had slipped out of Cherbourg. One landing ship was sunk and one badly damaged, and six hundred and thirty-nine US servicemen died. Of even greater concern for the planners of Operation Overlord was the fact that ten officers, who had knowledge of the plan, were missing. The possibility that they had been captured could not be ruled out, and the planners could only rest easily when all ten bodies had been found and accounted for. As the preparations for invasion approached, the Allied soldiers were confined to camps and as much effort as possible was made to prevent any slips. Further up the chain, however, there were one or two incidents which caused great alarm. One American General was relieved of his command when he casually informed other officers at a cocktail party that, *"the invasion would take place before June 15th"*. A British Colonel was similarly dismissed when he informed his friends that he was preparing his command, *"to go to Normandy."* The ordinary troops remained confined to their barracks and surrounded, in many cases, with both barbed wire and armed guards, so great were security precautions, as was later recalled by one veteran:

"You knew you were going somewhere in France because they paid us out in French Francs in these camps they put us all in before D-Day. They penned us all up before D-Day, all long the south coast, and we weren't allowed to go out to tell anyone where we were going. They paid us with little paper money, it was special invasion money. Most of the lads in camp didn't have nothing else to do so we were playing cards, so most of us lost our money."

THE ALLIED FORCES ENGAGED IN NORMANDY

Supreme Commander:
General Dwight Eisenhower

Deputy Supreme Commander:
Air Marshal Sir Arthur Tedder

Chief of Staff: Major-General
Walter Bedell Smith

Commander 21st Army Group:
General Sir Bernard
Montgomery

Commander US 1st Army Group:
Lieutenant-General
Omar Bradley

Commander Air
Expeditionary Force:
Air Chief Marshal
Sir Trafford Leigh-Mallory

Supreme Headquarters Allied Expeditionary Force (SHAEF)

Supreme Commander: General Dwight Eisenhower
Deputy Supreme Commander: Air Marshal Sir Arthur Tedder
Chief of Staff: Major-General Walter Bedell Smith

21st ARMY GROUP *
General Sir Bernard Montgomery

2nd BRITISH ARMY *
Lieutenant-General Sir Miles Dempsey
- I Corps (until 23rd July 1944).
  Commanded by Lieutenant-General
  JT Crocker *
- VIII Corps (from 16th July 1944).
  Commanded by Lieutenant-General
  Sir Richard O'Connor+
- XII Corps (from 30th June 1944).
  Commanded by Lieutenant-General
  NM Richie+
- XXX Corps. Commanded by
  Lieutenant-General BC Bucknall
  (until 3rd August 1944), then
  replaced by Lieutenant-General BG
  Horrocks *

Armoured Divisions
- 7 Armoured Division+
- Guards Armoured Division+
- 11 Armoured Division
- 79 Armoured Division *

Infantry Divisions
- 3 Division *
- 6 Airborne Division *
- 15 (Scottish) Division+
- 43 (Wessex) Division +
- 49 (West Riding) Division *
- 50 (Northumberland) Division *
- 51 (Highland) Division *
- 53 (Welsh) Division+
- 59 (Staffordshire) Division+

Independent Armoured Brigades
- 4 Armoured Brigade *
- 6 (Guards) Tank Brigade+
- 8 Armoured Brigade *
- 27 Armoured Brigade *

- 33 Armoured Brigade+
- 31 Tank Brigade+
- 34 Tank Brigade+

Independent Commando Brigades
- 1 Special Service Brigade *
- 4 Special Service Brigade *

1st CANADIAN ARMY
(from 23 July 1944) Commanded by+
Lieutenant-General HGC Crerar

II Canadian Corps (from 2nd British
Army 23rd July 1944). Commanded by
Lieutenant-General GS Simonds+

Independent Armoured Brigades
- 2 Canadian Armoured Brigade *

Armoured Divisions
- 4 Canadian Armoured Division+
- 1 Polish Armoured Division+

Infantry Divisions
- 2 Canadian Division+
- 3 Canadian Division *

US 12th ARMY GROUP+
(from 1st August 1944) Commanded by
Lieutenant-General Omar Bradley

1st US Army *
Lieutenant-General Omar Bradley (to
1st August 1944), then replaced by
Lieutenant-General Courtney Hodges

3rd US Army+ (from August 2nd)
Lieutenant-General George Patton Jr

Corps
- V Corps. Commanded by Major-General Leonard Gerow *
  Initially part of 21st Army group
- VII Corps (from 15th June 1944) Commanded by Major-General Troy Middleton *
- XII Corps (from 29 July 1944) Commanded by Major-General Gilbert Cook+
- XV Corps (from 2nd August 1944) Commanded by Major-General Wade Haislip+
- XIX Corps (from 12th June 1944) Commanded by Major-General Charles Corlett+
- XX Corps (from 2nd August 1944) Commanded by Major-General Walton Walker+

Infantry Divisions
- 1 Division *
- 2 Division+
- 4 Division *
- 5 Division+
- 8 Division+
- 9 Division *
- 28 Division+
- 29 Division *
- 35 Division+
- 79 Division *
- 80 Division+
- 82 Airborne Division *
- 83 Division+
- 90 Division *
- 101 Airborne Division *

Armoured Divisions
- 2 Armoured Division *
- 3 Armoured Division+
- 4 Armoured Division+
- 5 Armoured Division+
- 6 Armoured Division+
- 7 Armoured Division+
- 2 French Armoured Division+

ALLIED EXPEDITIONARY AIR FORCE
Air Chief Marshal
Sir Trafford Leigh-Mallory

RAF SECOND TACTICAL AIR FORCE *
Air Marshal Sir Arthur Coningham
- 73 fighter squadrons
- 20 medium bomber squadrons
- 7 army co-operation squadrons
Comprising approx 1,220 aircraft in total

US 9th AIR FORCE*
Lieutenant-General Lewis Brereton (to 7th August 1944), then replaced by Major-General Joyt Vandenberg
- 44 medium bomber squadrons
- 65 fighter squadrons
- 56 transport squadrons
Comprising approx 2,000 aircraft in total

RAF BOMBER COMMAND *
Air Chief Marshal Sir Arthur Harris
- 73 heavy bomber squadrons
- 15 light bomber squadrons
Comprising approx 1,400 aircraft

US 8TH AIR FORCE *
Lieutenant-General James Doolittle
- 160 heavy bomber squadrons
- 45 fighter squadrons
Comprising approx 2,400 aircraft

Note: Not all of the above units fought in the first wave on D-Day 6th June 1944. Many were introduced during the subsequent battles for Normandy which ended in the fall of Falaise in August 1944.

* Served as part of Twenty First Army Group in the first wave on June 6th 1944.
+ Arrived as reinforcements, or created after June 6th.

101

OPERATION FORTITUDE

False intelligence was also an important part of the build up to Operation Overlord. This required a mini-operation in its own right, which was given the code name of Fortitude, this consisted of an elaborate deception attempt to convince the Germans that the actual raid would take place in the Pas de Calais. False jetties, oil storage tanks, oil pipe lines, anti-aircraft guns and rows of tanks were created, in order to convince the few German aircraft which managed to slip through on reconnaissance missions, that the invasion was poised to strike at the Pas de Calais. In addition, a fictitious army group known as the US First Army was created, and it was given the task of filling the air with radio traffic. It certainly seemed to play its part which cannot be under-estimated, as the Germans actively began to believe that the real invasion would take place in the Pas de Calais. Fortitude played its part in the early stages of Overlord by creating confusion among the German high command, who were still uncertain that the operation itself was not a decoy operation.

THE ALLIED PLANS

As commander of Allied 21st Army Group, Field Marshal Bernard Montgomery had the enormous responsibility of leading the forces on the ground during the Normandy campaign of 1944. He set a very precise strategy for the campaign, as outlined at the meeting of senior commanders in St Paul's School, London, on May 15th, 1944.

It was intended that the four Allied corps which landed on the five beaches on D-Day would penetrate to a depth of about ten kilometres inland and capture the towns of the Bayeux and Caen. By D-Day plus ten, the Allies would have secured the line of high ground running from St Lô to Villers-Bocage. While the British engaged the German forces in a battle which was intended to be fought south of Caen, it was planned that Patton's third army would expand southwards in a grand encircling movement designed to trap the German forces, and by D-Day plus ninety the Allies would be encamped along the River Seine and Paris would be in their hands.

Present at the meeting at St Paul's School, where Montgomery outlined his strategy for the grand campaign, were King George VI, Winston Churchill and General Eisenhower, Supreme Commander of Allied forces in the West. Recalling the meeting some years after the event, the US General Omar Bradley was impressed by the selfless role which was assumed by the British Forces.

"The British and Canadian armies were to decoy the enemy reserves and draw them to their front on the extreme Eastern edge of the Allied beach heads. While Monty taunted the enemy at Caen we were to make our break out on a long roundabout road to Paris. When reckoned in terms of national pride, this British decoy mission became a sacrificial one, for while we tramped around on the outside flank, the British were to sit in place and pin down

Port Operating Headquarters staff land in Normandy. The logistical headaches are about to start for these men.

General Charles de Gaulle lands in France for the first time in four years on June 14th, 1944.

the Germans. Yet strategically, it fitted into a logical division of labours, for it was towards Caen that enemy forces would race once the alarm was sounded."

The British and Canadians by persistently attacking on either side of Caen posed the greatest threat of a breakout from Normandy, and the Germans always perceived this as the greatest danger. As it happened, this produced the situation in which, with the German armour grouped against the British and the Canadians, the break out came in the West from the Americans.

By committing his forces around Caen, Montgomery knew it was the British who would face the bulk of the German armour. Although new types of tank were beginning to reach the German forces, they still had to rely on older designs to fill the bulk of the Panzer divisions.

METICULOUS PLANNING

There can be few campaigns in the history of warfare which were as meticulously planned and so heavily insured against failure as the D-Day landings of 1944. The Anglo-American forces which stormed ashore on Hitler's Fortress Europe enjoyed an overwhelming superiority in men, ammunition, ships, tanks, planes, and all the rest of the panoply of war.

The 6th June 1944 would see two considerable armed forces pitted against one another in the Normandy area. 160,000 Allied troops in three airborne and five amphibiously landed infantry divisions were deployed in Normandy on 6th June against German defenders of varying quality, but still in considerable strength on the ground.

The amphibious landings of D-Day were mounted from Britain and they were very much a British Naval operation. Just under four out of every five of the ships involved in the operation were either British Royal Navy or they belonged to the navies of dominion and

Lieutenant-General Omar Bradley, Commanding General of the 12th Army Group (centre) seen here with Lieutenant-General Courtney H. Hoges (left), and Lieutenant-General George S. Patton (right).

imperial fleets. This applied just as much to the American landing beaches as it did to the British landing beaches. Only about one sixth of all the ships involved were actually from the American Navy.

In 1945 A.V. Alexander, first Lord of the Admiralty, describing the creation of the shipping required commented at the time:

Lieutenant-General Sir Miles Dempsey with Lieutenant-General Richard Nugent O'Connor (left).

"The Naval forces required for the assault landing consisted of four main classes: minesweepers, to clear the way for all the ships and craft which would follow; landing craft and ships of all kinds to carry the soldiers and the guns, tanks, transport and other equipment with which they would fight; bombarding ships, whose task, with the Air Force, would be to destroy the enemy's opposition to the landing, and enable the Army to gain the lodgement which it required before it could deploy its own weapons; and finally the escort and anti-submarine forces.

The minesweepers, bombarding ships and escort vessels already existed, though they were required in exceptionally large numbers.

The landing ships and craft did not exist. They have all had to be developed and provided during the war from our own resources and those of our Allies. The process was started as soon as the armies of the United Nations were driven from the Continent, very many months before it became fashionable to chalk up on the walls demands for a 'Second Front.'

While the Fleet with which we are familiar was still being built and maintained, this strange new Fleet, containing ships of all sizes and odd shapes, each designed and developed for its special purpose, was brought into being. It included ships and craft for landing tanks and infantry, for giving close support fire, for landing guns and transport, for making smoke, and even floating kitchens and craft fitted with extending fire escape ladders to put men up cliffs. In all, 4,066 landing ships and craft of over sixty different types took part in the operation.

Shore works costing several million pounds had to be provided before the assault could be launched."

- CHAPTER 5 -

THE GERMAN FORCES

On the other side of the Atlantic, the Germans knew that the invasion was coming. There was no doubt that the war could be won only by the opening of a second front, which had to be in France. The German forces in Italy, despite difficult conditions had done a tenacious job of stalling the Allied advance, and further progress looked like a costly and slow affair. They had also made considerable steps in the preparation of what Hitler optimistically called the Atlantic Wall, which was intended to assure the protection of the coast from the Arctic to Spain. Work had actually began on the Atlantic Wall in 1942, and, using slave labour supplied by the hated TODT organisation, it was considerably advanced by early 1944. Although it was not complete, there were still numerous concrete gun emplacements and block houses which dotted the coastline. But it was certainly not a continuous line. In places which were more susceptible to invasion, mines and obstacles covered the beaches, and the defences from the Dutch German border to the Loire River were especially formidable. This was the sector of Army Group B, commanded from January 1944 by Field Marshal Erwin Rommel.

On the German side, the Allied air superiority was just one of a number of serious disadvantages which had to be overcome if they were to conduct a successful campaign in Normandy. Chief among these was the confusion and disorganisation which prevailed in the chain of command. As supreme commander, Adolf Hitler constantly dabbled in every aspect of the forces at his command, and he had a habit of reserving particularly powerful formations for his personal control.

The situation in France was a particularly complicated one. The nominal Commander in Chief was von Runstedt, who controlled Army Group B, responsible for northern France and Belgium, and

Army Group G which was responsible for southern France; but Rommel in command of Army Group B enjoyed the favour of Hitler and in practice could not be overruled by his superiors. To further compound matters, three of the Panzer divisions operating within Rommel's area of influence were allocated to a separate formation known as Panzer Group West. This powerful grouping was designated as an Army Reserve and could be deployed only on the express authority of Hitler himself. This complicated and divisive policy was a result of Hitler's mistrust of the generals, and there is a great deal of evidence to suggest that the 'divide and rule' policy was a deliberate stratagem on Hitler's part.

The Sturmgeschutze was an effective tank destroyer which was introduced into service in this variant, in 1942. The long barrelled 75mm anti-tank gun was soon proved to be effective against the Russian T-34. It was equally effective against the Allied Sherman tanks.

THE GERMAN FORCES ENGAGED IN NORMANDY

Commander in Chief:
Adolf Hitler

Chief of Staff:
Generalfelfmarschall
Wilhelm Keitel

Chief of Operations Staff:
Generaloberst
Alfred Jodl

Generalfeldmarschall
Gerd von Rundstedt

Generalfeldmarschall
Günter von Kluge

Luftwaffe Commander-in-Chief:
Reichsmarschall
Hermann Goering

Oberkommando der Wehrmacht (OKW)

Commander in Chief: Adolf Hitler
Chief of Staff: Generalfelfmarschall Wilhelm Keitel
Chief of Operations Staff: Generaloberst Alfred Jodl

OBERBEFELSHABER WEST
(OB WEST) *
Generalfeldmarschall Gerd von
Rundstedt (to 2nd July 1944), then
replaced by Generalfeldmarschall
Günter von Kluge (to 18th
August 1944), then replaced by
Generalfeldmarschall Walther Model

ARMY GROUP B *
Generalfeldmarschall Erwin Rommel
(to 17th July 1944), then replaced by
Generalfeldmarschall Gunther von
Kluge (to 18th August 1944), then
replaced by Generalfeldmarschall
Walther Model

SEVENTH ARMY *
Generaloberst Friedrich Dollmann
(to 28th June 1944), then replaced by
Oberstgruppenführer Paul Hausser (to
20th August 1944), then replaced by
General der Panzertruppen Heinrich
Eberbach (to 30th August 1944)

PANZER GROUP WEST (to 5th
August 1944)+ FIFTH PANZER
ARMY+
General der Panzertruppen Leo
Freiherr Geyr von Schweppenburg
(to 6th July 1944), then replaced by
General der Panzertruppen Heinrich
Eberbach (to 9th August 1944), then
replaced by Oberstgruppenführer
Joseph 'Sepp' Dietrich
  • I SS Panzer Corps+
    Obergruppenführer Joseph 'Sepp'
    Dietrich (to 9th August 1944), then
    replaced by Obergruppenführer
    Hermann Priess

  • II SS Panzer Corps+
    Obergruppenfuhrer Paul Hausser
    (to 28 July 1944), then replaced
    by Obergruppenfuhrer Wilheim
    Bittrich
  • XLVII Panzer Corps *
    General der Panzertruppen Hans
    Freiherr von Funck
  • LVIII Panzer Corps+
    General der Panzertruppen Waiter
    Kruger
  • II Parachute Corps+
    General der Falschirmtruppen
    Eugen Meindl
  • XXV Corps+
    General der Artillerie Wilhelm
    Fahrmbacher
  • LXXIV Corps+
    General der Infanterie Erich
    Straube
  • LXXX1 Corps+
    General der Panzertruppen Adolf
    Kuntzen
  • LXXXIV Corps+
    General der Artillerie Erich Marcks
    (to 12th June 1944), then replaced
    by General der Artillerie Wilhelm
    Fahrmbacher, (to 18th June 1944)
    then replaced by Generalleutnant
    Dietrich von Choltitz (to 28th
    July 1944), then replaced by
    Generalleutnant Otto Elfeldt
  • LXXXIV Corps+
    General der Infanterie Hans von
    Obstfelder

PANZER DIVISIONS
  • 2 Panzer Division+
  • 9 Panzer Division+
  • 21 Panzer Division *
  • 116 Panzer Division+
  • 'Panzer Lehr' Division+

WAFFEN-SS DIVISIONS
- 1 SS Panzer Division 'Leibstandarte Adolf Hitler'+
- 2 SS Panzer Division 'Das Reich'+
- 9 SS Panzer Division 'Hohenstauffen'+
- 10 SS Panzer Division 'Frundsberg'+,
- 12 SS Panzer Division 'Hitler Jugend'+
- 17 SS Panzergrenadier Division 'Goetz von Berlichingen'+

INDEPENDENT SCHWERE PANZER BATTALIONS
- 101 SS Heavy Tank Battalion+
- 102 SS Heavy Tank Battalion+
- 10 Heavy Tank Battalion, (later renumbered 501-503 Heavy Tank Battalion)+

INDEPENDENT SCHWERE PANZERJAEGER BATTALIONS
- 654 Heavy Anti-Tank Battalion+
- 668 Heavy Anti-Tank Battalion+
- 709 Anti-Tank Battalion+

INFANTRY DIVISIONS
- 77 Division+
- 84 Division+
- 85 Division+
- 89 Division+
- 243 Static Division+
- 265 Static Division+
- 266 Static Division+
- 271 Division+
- 272 Division+
- 275 Division+
- 276 Division+
- 277 Division+
- 326 Static Division+
- 331 Division+
- 343 Static Division+
- 344 Static Division+
- 346 Static Division+
- 352 Division *
- 353 Division+
- 363 Division+
- 709 Static Division *
- 711 Static Division *
- 716 Static Division *

INDEPENDENT ARTILLERY BRIGADES
- 7 Werfer Brigade+
- 8 Werfer Brigade+
- 9 Werfer Brigade+

LUFTWAFFE DIVISIONS
- 2 Parachute Division+
- 3 Parachute Division+
- 5 Parachute Division+
- 16 Luftwaffe Field Division+
- 91 Airlanding Division *

OBERKOMMANDO DER LUFTWAFFE (OKL)
Commander-in-chief: Reichsmarschall Hermann Goering

LUFTFLOTTE 3 *
Generalfeldmarschall Hugo Sperrie

	Aircraft establishment
Day fighters	315
Night fighters	90
Bombers	402
Transport	64

NB. In practice, aircraft strength may have been up to 40% lower.

- Ill Flak Corps *
- Approx 460 anti-aircraft guns of various calibre

Not all of the above units fought on D-Day 6th June 1944. Many were introduced during the subsequent battles for Normandy which ended in the fall of Falaise in August 1944. Many units were moved between the various corps and Army Groups.

* Units engaged on June 6th.
+ Units created or committed after June 6th.

HITLER'S POLICY

Adolf Hitler believed in struggle; that the strongest man would emerge from a natural process of struggle, and he organised the Nazi state that way. The German command structure was, in effect, not set up to co-operate with itself, but rather as a series of competing structures which were meant to fight each other. In some respects they did this so well that they defeated themselves as well as the Allies fighting them in Normandy. The command structure was farcical. As we have seen, commanding all the forces in the west, responsible for France, Belgium and Holland was Obercommando West, based in Paris, under the sixty-nine year old Field Marshal Gerd von Runstedt. He was officially in charge of Army Group B, which was responsible for the defence of Normandy, and which was commanded by Field Marshal Erwin Rommel. But at the same time, Rommel was effectively von Runstedt's superior by dint of the fact that Rommel had a watching brief from Hitler for the defence for the whole of western Europe. Rommel, who was one of Hitler's

A wounded German prisoner is led past under the interested gaze of a British paratrooper on the first day of 'Overlord'. Scenes like this would soon become commonplace.

favourites, had direct access to Hitler, which von Runstedt did not enjoy. He still had to work his way through the labyrinthine German hierarchy to reach the Fuhrer.

The son of Field Marshal Montgomery later recalled the advantages which the confused German hierarchy offered to the forces led by his father.

"I think the German command was a very confused structure leading up to Hitler himself, who insisted on taking many of even the small decisions himself. There was no doubt about it that this impeded the efficiency of the German generals. My father had an enormous respect for the German High Command and indeed for the German army as a whole. He had fought them in two wars and fought in the desert, and had very high regard for their efficiency, discipline and their skill at arms. As a result, of course, he knew who he was facing, knew quite a lot about them, studied them very carefully, and I think that the fact that they had this rather laborious chain of command back to Hitler, was a factor which played in our favour, because Hitler was a complete megalomaniac who tended to try and instruct the generals what they should do against their own better judgement."

This was this quite deliberate confusion, two Field Marshals competing with each other for control over the German organisation. It reached a critical point with the control of the German armoured reserves, Panzer group West. Rommel believed that the only chance for defeating the Allied invasion was to do so on the D-Day beaches and drive it into the sea. The famous phrase of his Chief of Staff, which Rommel adopted, was that this would be the *'longest day'*. What Rommel meant was, if the Allies were allowed, at the end of D-Day, still to be ashore, then Allied strength was such that victory in the Battle of Normandy would be inevitable and there was nothing the Germans could do. Rommel therefore wanted the armoured reserves as close to the beaches as possible for a quick counter attack.

Von Runstedt disagreed with Rommel's strategy. His view was

very much the same as that which Montgomery correctly foresaw, that the best German strategy would be to fight a slow withdrawal battle inland. For that reason, von Runstedt wanted the armoured reserves held back until he could properly appraise the situation and mount the appropriate response.

The compromise was utterly unrealistic; it produced a plan which was neither fish nor fowl. Some of the German armoured divisions were close to the beaches, while others were placed far inland. In any event, none of them could be moved without Hitler's own permission. This muddle was to produce the famous circumstance on D-Day itself, when von Runstedt, desperate to move his armoured forces, was told that Hitler was sleeping and could not be wakened. His own Chief of Staff finally suggested to von Runstedt that if

A young German soldier from one of the ordinary Wehrmacht divisions. This pathetic image gives a lasting impression of just how young many of the 'men' in the ranks actually were. This youngster can be no more than sixteen years of age.

he himself got on the phone and insisted that they wake Hitler, he might obtain the Fuhrer's permission. Von Runstedt, a sixty-nine year old Prussian aristocrat, simply could not bring himself to ring this 'bohemian corporal', Adolf Hitler, and he refused to do so, with predictable consequences.

The struggles in the Wehrmacht hierarchy were merely the start of the problems for the Germans on D-Day. In addition to the dual command, as with von Runstedt and Rommel being in dispute over who commanded the army, there were separate command chains for the German airforce, the Luftwaffe divisions, which included many of the dual-purpose anti-aircraft guns, and the crucial 88mm guns, which were vital for anti-tank defence. It was not unusual for Luftwaffe commanders to refuse to take orders from the German army officers, on the grounds they were still not in the same service.

In addition, the Luftwaffe had its own field divisions and its own parachute divisions. None of them were really capable of making a

Some of the German self-propelled artillery which served in Normandy was manufactured from the chassis of captured French vehicles.

Young German soldiers pose for the Allied cameras in the aftermath of the Normandy Battles. The extreme youth of many of those who formed the German armies is amply demonstrated by this group.

Many of the German divisions fighting in Normandy had experience of combat from other fronts. These grenadiers, wearing camouflage netting on their helmets, suggest an air of confidence.

drop by this stage of the war, but they were not strictly speaking, under army command.

The Kriegsmarine, the German navy, also had its separate chain of command; there was no formal co-ordination with the army. The Waffen SS, under Heindrich Himmler, which by this stage of the war consisted of ten armoured divisions and a further twenty infantry divisions, also has its separate chain of command. Co-ordination was poor. Even within the Wehrmacht units there were communication problems, even between armies. The 15th Army, just to the north of where the Normandy landings would take place, had a very good intelligence officer who had actually cracked some of the codes for D-Day and was aware in the early hours that the landings were about to take place. Because his army was not communicating effectively with the 7th Army, however, no alert was received. With friends like this the Germans did not need enemies as good as the Allies.

THE GERMAN FORCES

The German command and control system has been described by one author as fragmented and muddled, and if anything this rather understates the case. The German command structure in Normandy, and indeed Western Europe as a whole by 1944, was a confused, almost amorphous mess, for reasons which have a great deal to do with Hitler's desire to set Germany's institutions, including the armed forces, against one another as part of a rather perverted idea of social Darwinism. As we have seen, the army, Waffen SS, navy and Luftwaffe units all operated within different and often contradictory or competing command structure. This certainly made the German prosecution of any successful counter attack or counter offensive, once the Allies landed in Normandy, much less likely to succeed than might otherwise have been the case, had they had a clear and coherent command structure.

Inside a German self-propelled gun. Ammunition supply was a crucial consideration and the German forces had to be careful to conserve their ammunition.

HANDBOOK ON GERMAN MILITARY FORCES
EXTRACT NO.10
INFANTRY TANK CO-OPERATION

"....When the enemy has well prepared positions with natural or constructed tank obstacles, the German infantry attacks before the tanks and clears the way. The objective of the infantry is to penetrate into the enemy position and destroy enemy antitank weapons, augmented by additional support and covering fire from the tanks and self-propelled weapons sited in their rear.

Only after the destruction of the enemy anti-tank defence can the tanks be employed on the battle line to the fullest advantage.

When the tank obstacles in front of the enemy position are destroyed, and no additional tank obstacles are expected in the depth of the enemy's main defensive position, the infantry breaks through simultaneously with the tank unit. The infantry attack is conducted in the same manner as it would be without the co-operation of tanks. Heavy infantry weapons are kept in readiness to fire at possible, newly discovered anti-tank positions. Of particular importance is protection of the open flanks by echeloning the flank units and employing heavy weapons at the flanks.

In most cases, the infantry follows the tanks closely, taking advantage of the fire power and paralysing effect of the tanks upon the enemy's defence. The Germans normally transport the infantry to the line of departure on tanks or troop-carrying vehicles in order to protect the infantry and to increase its speed. The infantry leaves the vehicles at the last possible moment, and goes into action mainly with light automatic weapons.

The tanks advance by bounds from cover to cover, reconnoitering the terrain ahead and providing protective fire for the dismounted Panzer Grenadiers. The tanks do not slow their advance to enable the infantry to keep continuous pace with them, but advance alone and wait under cover until the infantry catches up with the advance. Terrain that does not offer sufficient cover is crossed with the greatest possible speed.

The infantry attacks in small formations also by bounds under the fire cover of its own heavy weapons and of the tanks, staying away from individual tanks because they draw the strongest enemy fire.

When a tank company attacks with infantry, there are normally two platoons on the line, one platoon back, and the fourth platoon in reserve. The interval between tanks is usually one hundred to one hundred and twenty yards. The tank's machine guns usually engage infantry targets at about a thousand yards range and under, while the tank guns engage targets at two thousand to two thousand five hundred yards.

The co-ordination between tanks and Panzer Grenadiers moving into combat on armoured half-tracks is similar to the technique employed in a purely armoured formation, since the armoured halftracks are not only troop-carrying vehicles but also combat vehicles. When the terrain is favourable for tank warfare, the Panzer Grenadiers in their armoured half-tracks follow immediately with the second wave, after the first tank wave has overrun the opponent's position. A deep and narrow formation is employed. After the penetration, the main mission of the Panzer Grenadiers is to overcome the enemy positions which survived the first wave....."

TIGER
(Kpfw VI TIGER I AUSF H/E)

Probably the most famous tank to emerge from World War Two was the Tiger. This vehicle represented a quantum leap forward in tank design. First produced in 1942 in response to the demand for heavy tanks, it first went into combat at Leningrad in August 1942. In Normandy, as in Russia, the Tiger was never available in sufficient quantities to effect the outcome of the battle.

Many of the units in Rommel's army group are very often admired for their fighting ability and there is no doubt that the best of the divisions, especially the armoured divisions, the Panzer Divisions, were very good indeed. Whereas the Allies enjoyed good logistical back up behind the fighting divisions, with extremely good transport and supply, the Germans had a handful of good, well supplied units and a large number of units which were under strength, poorly equipped, with poor transport. As for the idea of the

German fighting 'Superman', about one in ten in Rommel's Army Group B was not actually German and in the front lines on D-Day, manning the pillbox positions, that proportion may have been as high as one in four. These were men who were volunteers from various countries occupied by the Germans, or prisoners of war, particularly from the Asiatic republics of the Soviet Union, who were simply taken and used quite deliberately, it would appear, as cannon fodder to be in the front line for D-Day.

"There is a letter written by my father to a friend of his in the War Office on the 8th June detailing the strange assortment of prisoners which were taken in the first two days of the Normandy campaign. Prisoners came from all the Asiatic republics of the Soviet Union, as well as Poles, Latvians, and an incredible mixture of other nationalities. Two were even listed as Japanese. It was assumed at the time that these were simply Japanese observers with the Germans, who had got caught up in the action. When it was

Young SS men captured in the immediate aftermath of the Normandy landings. The average age of the Hitler Jugend SS division was officially given as eighteen - in practice there were a fair number in the ranks who were much younger.

found they didn't speak Japanese or any other known language, a linguistic expert was summoned, he discovered who they were; in fact they were two Tibetan shepherds. According to their story they had been taken prisoner up on the Tibetan plateau by what must have been Soviet forces, put into Soviet uniforms, taken somewhere 'which wasn't Tibet'. There they had been captured by people in grey uniforms, Germans, and taken somewhere else, 'which wasn't Tibet', Montgomery recalled that they were very impressed about how big that river was out there, but they were delighted to be taken prisoner by the British, who on the whole, they thought quite highly of, their final request was, "could we please go home now!"

THE HITLER YOUTH DIVISION

The 12th SS Panzer Division, Hitler Jugend, better known as the Hitler Youth Division, was formed in July 1943 from seventeen year old recruits in the training camps. These were boys who were seven years old when Hitler came to power, and in consequence they had never known any other life than that under the Nazi regime.

It was formed as the living embodiment and continuation of the Nazi and SS ideology, the representation of the future and as a symbol of the commitment of German youth to die for the Fuhrer. There can be little doubt that the German high authorities in late 1943-early 1944 knew perfectly well the Second World War was lost; to take these seventeen and eighteen year old boys full of ideological spirit and to commit them to die in Normandy against the Allies has been described as an act of 'almost grotesque barbarism'.

The Hitler Youth Division was virtually unique in the German order of battle in the Normandy campaign. Composed of utterly fanatical, ideologically dedicated young Nazis, with an average age of eighteen, the Hitler Youth Division was to prove itself as perhaps one of the most effective fighting formations available to the Germans. It was extremely well equipped as a full strength

Members of the Hitler Youth parade in Berlin early in 1944.

SS Panzer Division, and its personnel were not only ideologically committed but were also extremely well trained. Furthermore, they were extremely well led. Most of the officers and the NCOs of the Hitler Youth Division in fact came from the 1st SS Panzer Division, the Leibstandarte, which had had an enormous amount of experience by 1944. As such it was to prove a real thorn in the side of the Allied armies in Normandy, and some particularly savage fighting occurred between the Canadians and the Hitler Youth Division early on in the battle for Normandy.

Vera Duckworth served as a nurse in Normandy and recalled the awful fate of some of these youngsters:

"The Normandy campaign was really very distressing, all these young chaps coming back, just terrible wounds and you could only just patch them up enough to get them shipped back to England. We were very sad to see these young German prisoners of war, boys of about sixteen coming in with gangrenous feet, needing amputation, it seemed very wicked. They were so badly wounded and so young."

PANTHER
(PzKpfw V)

Arguably the best known and most outstanding German tank of World War Two. Only 3,740 Panzer V (AUSF G) models were produced between March 1944 and April 1945, compared to 20,000 Allied Shermans and 22,000 Russian T-34s.

The Hitler Jugend Division in battle behaved differently from many other troops and sometimes caught the Allies by surprise. They were very determined, very aggressive, much more likely to get themselves killed. There are accounts of Hitler Youth Soldiers running up to tanks and holding a sticky bomb against the tank with their body until it exploded. This of course meant their casualty rates were extremely high. The division was effectively wiped out in Normandy and later had to be reconstituted; the divisional commander was also killed and his replacement, Kurt Meyer, was wounded.

Since they had never been taught of the possibility of defeat

A member of the Hitler Youth Division is taken into captivity in the aftermath of the Normandy battles. Although the Hitler Youth Division fought very well in the campaign, they could not escape the inevitable end which awaited them.

or surrender, they also had no idea what was accepted practice regarding prisoners. Name, rank and number was not a drill with which the Hitler Jugend were familiar. As prisoners they were quite likely to ask for a map and provide through a detailed account of the engagement, explaining how well everybody had done, which was frequently a marvellous source of information for Allied intelligence.

At the end of the war in Europe, in a prisoner of war camp, the commander of the Hitler Jugend quite seriously volunteered to recreate an SS division for the Allies, to go out to the far east and fight the Japanese to show them how it was really done.

GERMAN ARMOUR

While it is true to say that the best of the German formations in the Normandy battle were considerably better than the best of the Allied formations, it should be borne in mind that many others were substandard. One area in which the Germans had a real advantage was in the quality of their tanks.

Not only were the crews hugely experienced and battle hardened by years on the Russian front, the tanks themselves were far better than those used by the Allies. In particular the Tiger, Panther and the new King Tiger tanks could all engage Allied tanks at much longer ranges than those at which the Allies could fight back. The superior armour of the tanks also gave the Germans a marked advantage in battle. Time and time again Allied tank soldiers described that disheartening experience of seeing their own shells bounce off the armour of the German tanks. This disparity in quality was to have a very real impact on the coming battles.

The relative disadvantage of the Allied soldiers fighting against German armour was realised by the son of Field Marshal Montgomery.

"I feel throughout the entire war that we were generally always

fighting with inferior equipment, and I think this is one of the demonstrations of the skill of both the Allied command and the qualities of the British soldier despite the fact that we had inferior equipment in many cases, and we were able to succeed."

One of the few dissenting voices on this topic was heard in 1945. Politicians are less likely to speak honestly than fighting men, and this extract from a speech in the House of Commons in 1945 by Sir James Grigg is peculiar, as it gives a very unorthodox view of the relative qualities of the tank forces. It is interesting to note, too, that Montgomery is quoted as a source:

"Let me say a little about tanks. First as regards guns. The Royal Tiger, alone of the enemy's tanks, mounts a gun - a hardened tip 88mm, firing a 22.5lb shot, with a muzzle velocity of 3,340 feet per second has a penetrative performance superior to that of our 17-pounder firing conventional shot. The standard 88mm mounted

The tense face of a grenadier as he awaits a potential Allied attack in the close confines of the Bocage. He carries with him a Panzerfaust anti-tank grenade, which made infantry very effective against tank attack.

in the ordinary Tiger and the 75mm mounted in the Panther are both inferior weapons. But the 17-pounder firing the latest type of ammunition surpasses the performance of any German gun yet encountered or, so far as I know, in contemplation. Moreover, we have in action at least five tanks mounting a 17-pounder for every Royal Tiger the Germans have on the Western Front.

Then as to armour - it is true that the frontal thickness of the Tigers and indeed of the Panther makes them all three formidable offensive weapons. But we aren't any longer fighting a defensive war. Field-Marshal Montgomery himself thinks that British armour has come through the campaign in Western Europe with flying colours, and has proved itself superior in battle to German armour. He holds that if Runstedt had been equipped with British armour when he attacked in the Ardennes on December 16th, he would have reached the Meuse in thirty-six hours, which would have placed the Allies in a very awkward situation. And further that if the 21st Army Group had been equipped with German armour it could not have crossed

Even in 1944, a very high proportion of German transport was still horse drawn, a fact which was later noted by many of the British and American veterans. This field kitchen had been attacked by Allied fighter bombers some days before this picture was taken.

the Seine on August 28th, and reached Brussels on September 3rd and Antwerp on September 4th, thus cutting off the whole Pas de Calais area in eight days: which the Field-Marshal holds to be a very remarkable achievement with far-reaching results."

The more conventional view is that tanks like the German Tiger or the Panther were extremely modern and highly effective designs in 1944. The Tiger, for example, mounted the lethal 88mm gun and the Panther by 1944 at last, benefited from relatively reliable mechanics, and an effective 75mm anti-tank gun backed up by good sloped armour. It should be emphasised, however, that the majority of German tanks in Normandy were not Tigers and Panthers. They were in fact the rather obsolescent model, the Panzer IV, which had been around since the late 1930's in one form or another.

In addition, the Germans had quite large numbers of assault guns and a variety of tank destroyers in Normandy, but these were of variable quality, ranging from the excellent Jagdpanther, to the obsolete Marder series.

It is certainly true to say that tanks like the American Sherman and the British Cromwell and Churchill, were tank for tank not the equal of the best of the German tanks. Nonetheless, when up-gunned, the Sherman Firefly, which carried a 17lb anti-tank gun, could certainly engage the majority of the German tanks on relatively equal terms, and given that there were more than enough of them, they could overwhelm the better German tanks by sheer force of numbers.

TRANSPORT AND LOGISTICS

Consumption of petrol and ammunition tends to be higher in static than mobil operations. Supply was a massive headache for the Germans from the 6th of June onwards.

The continued presence of horse drawn transport was a shock to many Allied troops and it is often overlooked in discussions of the Normandy campaign:

"I remember once we went out on a recce into no-mans-land and we went down a road, it was absolutely strewn with telephone and electrical wires everywhere, we were stepping amongst these wires going down the road to this little village. There were dead horses that were still harnessed to the German guns and I was so surprised to see that the Germans were still using horses to draw their artillery into battle and they were still harnessed up to the guns at the side of the road where they had been hit, killed."

Ammunition supply was a problem for the Germans, with the Allied airforces bombing and destroying bridges. There were to be a number of occasions, for example, in which the 88mm anti-tank guns simply ran out of shells at a critical moment. When the Allied break out started and the Germans needed to assemble armoured reserves to counter-attack quickly and seal up the breach, the shortages of fuel and ammunition would become critical. They were also to experience that nightmare for armoured commanders, tanks running dry on the battlefield.

One of the very few King Tigers to reach the battlefront in Normandy. This tank had a very similar profile to the Panther, and in consequence, Panther tanks were frequently mistaken for the King Tiger, an understandable reaction for nervous men in a dangerous situation. The actual numbers of King Tigers engaged in Normandy may have been as low as two machines.

THE ARMY STRUCTURE

Very much in keeping with the ideology of the Nazi state, the German army was structured with too many combat divisions when compared to the support services and the transport services. This caused it considerable problems in the Battle of Normandy and elsewhere. By 1944 the Wehrmacht was also running out of trained reserves and trained troops.

The Allied ability to control the air and prevent the Germans from moving forces into Normandy, plus the general shortages, meant that in the coming battle, as long as the Germans obeyed Hitler's orders, and held their position, they would lose on average two thousand troops a day more than they could replace. That continued in a relentless attrition battle for almost two months until the German army broke.

The logistic deficiencies of the German forces in the battle for Normandy are still a matter for some dispute. At first glance the nature of the close-quarter fighting in which the Germans were involved for much of the campaign meant that the need for large petrol supplies was potentially rather less than might have been the case with large sweeping manoeuvres which characterised the war in Russia. However as vehicles move infrequently in positional fighting, mainly in low gear, petrol consumption can be very high. More ammunition is also used holding a position than in mobile operations. Furthermore, there were to be only very few cases of the Germans actually running out of ammunition at genuinely critical moments. Nonetheless, when the Allied break-out had began to materialise at the end of July and into August 1944, the inability of the Germans to provide large quantities of petrol for their tanks and other vehicles would badly damage their ability to launch any significant counter-stroke against the Allies as they broke through.

The overwhelming demands of a war on three fronts posed hosts of additional problems for the German logistics and supply system. Allied fighters and fighter-bombers had not restricted their attacks just to the troops on the ground, they also carried out a massive air interdiction campaign against the German supply lines. Roads and railway lines were mercilessly targeted, which meant that supplies of essential fuel and ammunition stocks could not reach the hard-pressed front line. By this stage of the war Germany was under constant attack by Allied bomber formations, and fuel was already in very short supply. In Normandy, fuel shortages became almost endemic and in many cases German tanks which were needed urgently to resist the invasion could not move through lack of fuel. The ceaseless Allied attacks on the long columns of fuel lorries served only to compound these problems.

THE PANZER DIVISIONS

To offset the many disadvantages which faced the German troops fighting on the ground in Normandy, they did enjoy some real advantages over the Allies in terms of experience. Many of the

Despite the ominous signs, most of the officer corps remained remarkably loyal to Hitler.

Sixty-four JU52 transports were available to Luftflotte 3 serving the German armies in Normandy. In Russia, these aircraft had been used to assist beleaguered forces, and could, in theory, have been used to alleviate supply difficulties. It was impossible, however, for these cumbersome machines to manoeuvre in the confined spaces of Normandy.

Panzer divisions which would be used to face the Allies had a strong core of battle-hardened, experienced troops, who had already seen four years of brutal warfare. This experience gave them the mental toughness which would serve them in great stead during the coming battle.

THE ATLANTIC WALL

On the debit side the entire Atlantic front was simply too long to be adequately defended and priority therefore had to be given to the most likely areas for invasion. There was still a number of these and the German forces, already spread thin, were constantly weakened by the needs of the Russian front. Hitler constantly took German divisions away from the task of defending the Atlantic Wall to shore up the crumbling front in the east.

In consequence, many of the divisions which were dispatched to the Atlantic Wall were poor quality and in some cases, actually comprised of troops who would have otherwise been considered unfit for service. The most famous example was the Stomach Battalions which were entirely composed of men with stomach complaints and who needed special diets. Nonetheless, in among these divisions were one or two very formidable formations such as the SS Leibstandarte and the Panzer Lehr Division. Both of these formations were to fight very hard indeed in the coming battle.

Dr Simon Trew comments: *"The battle experience of the German forces in Normandy varied dramatically between formations. Some units, for example the 1st SS Panzer Division, the Leibstandarte, were extremely experienced and battle hard and indeed well equipped. Others, for example, the 12th SS Panzer Division, the Hitler Youth Division, were very well equipped but utterly inexperienced. Many of the German divisions of course fell somewhere in between these two."*

Four years of savage warfare in Russia had drained the strength of the German army away.

For the duration of the Normandy campaign, only twenty per cent of the available German forces could be committed to the war in the West. The remaining eighty per cent had to be split between the five per cent needed to defend Germany territory in Italy and the seventy-five per cent which were always required to prevent the Russians from achieving a strategic victory in the East.

As we have seen, one of the great successes of the Normandy campaign was the secrecy with which the whole operation was shrouded.

The Germans were completely deceived as to the place and date of the landings, right up to the moment the first troops came ashore.

The Allies enjoyed the benefits of a steady flow of accurate information on enemy dispositions, which came from a highly efficient Allied spy network and from the eager efforts of the French Resistance, who constantly monitored the German troop movements and passed detailed information to London. In the air the Allies had an even greater advantage.

- CHAPTER 6 -

THE ALLIED JUGGERNAUT

The chief factor which makes the Battle of Normandy important is that German resources, by June 1944, were tremendously overstretched. Hitler had no real strategic reserves, therefore by opening up the long awaited, 'Second Front', and by forcing the Germans to commit their troops to Normandy, the final overstretch which broke the back of the German armed forces was achieved. In effect, this meant that the battle of Normandy, although small in scale compared to the giant battles on the eastern front, was nevertheless, one of the critical battles of the war.

THE NAVAL BOMBARDMENT

During the D-Day landings, and for up to twenty miles inland, the Allied forces could rely on the massive guns of the Allied battleships, which were capable of firing devastating barrages of heavy artillery fire against the German forces.

Even for those Germans who had fought in Russia, naval gunfire proved to be a devastating experience which was shocking in its intensity. The power of the heavy shells from the sixteen inch guns of the battleships, produced a barrage which was so intense, that Tiger tanks which weighed fifty-six tons, were flipped on to their sides like children's toys. In the opening days of the Normandy campaign, the Allies could rely upon the support of nine battleships, twenty-three cruisers and seventy-three destroyers. Many veterans recalled the terrific bombardment. Among them was Stan Watson:

"I was actually on Sword beach, just off Le Havre. At the start there was a terrific bombardment by the artillery, the Germans were pounded to bits. At the time I was pleased but, having said

that, I have been back there since, two or three times since, and when I go into the cemeteries there, it hits me now. Lads of about eighteen, lying there when it could have been you. It was a powerful experience, you know. We don't want it to happen again, that's all I can say."

Cyril Timms was aboard the Allied fleet as the bombardment began. More than fifty-five years later he can still vividly recall the effects of the shelling:

"When we were bombarding Normandy, we were anchored at Le Havre. We were bombarding twenty miles inland, a place called Caen. Incredible. We were being controlled, gunnery wise, by a spotter plane, twenty miles away. I don't know what the Germans thought, I'm sure. It certainly kept them on their feet when we put a few big shells amongst them.

The number of ships in the Channel that day was absolutely phenomenal. Thousands and thousands. The sea was black with ships. I'm surprised there weren't more collisions. There literally were thousands and thousands, and the sky was black with aircraft

Lancaster bombers of the RAF set out on another raid against occupied Europe. The overwhelming air superiority available to the Allies was used both in the strategic role to devastate German industry and, nearer to D-Day, as a means of attacking defences and providing interdiction against reinforcement.

Airborne troops aboard a glider. The British drop zone was just to the North of Caen where they were able to overcome the German resistance. American paratroops who landed near Carentan faced much stiffer defences and sustained very heavy casualties.

as well. I'm surprised they didn't have more accidents in the air than on the sea.

All the Allied ships were marked, as were the aircraft, with three stripes down each wing at that particular time. RAF, the ships and aircraft, were easily identified by these markings. I have never seen so many ships in my life. I think an awful lot of accidents happened as a result of that - it wasn't difficult to hit something else other than what you intended to.

We came under attack several times but we weren't hit actually on the D-Day, but coming back to refuel and reload with armaments we hit a mine off the Isle of Wight and that threw the ship into confusion; a gaping great hole in the side."

This vast assemblage had been brought to bear against an enemy which in many respects was already on the brink of defeat. At sea the Kriegsmarine could do almost nothing to impede the Allied fleet.

Of forty-five German U-boats ordered to strike at the Allied fleet, thirty were sunk, with only minimal losses in the D-Day Armada.

Already, before D-Day, the Allies had secured control of the English Channel, otherwise the invasion could simply not have taken place. The German naval response to D-Day itself would prove absolutely ineffective. Of the two fleets of light craft based at Cherbourg to the west and Le Havre to the east, the Cherbourg flotillas could not come out to sea because of the very bad weather conditions, which of course affected the Allied landings as well. In the east a small number of E-Boats which the Germans called S-Boats or Schnell boaten, these light torpedo craft did actually come out from Le Havre, but they were easily driven off by British destroyers.

Effectively there was no German naval response to D-Day. As the month of June progressed there was some German interference, with submarines and light craft operating against the forces coming across the Channel, but this never amounted to any significant danger to the Allied forces.

Two Spitfires on patrol over Southern Europe in 1943. The air cover given to the attacking ships and infantry in Normandy was almost complete. It was virtually impossible for the few German fighters to penetrate the screen of Allied fighters.

ALLIED AIR SUPERIORITY

The Allies had absolute control of the air for the Battle of Normandy. As we have seen, from April 1944 they had been conducting bombing operations against French targets including railway marshalling yards and bridges, forcing the Germans to commit their fighters to defend these targets and then engaging fighter to fighter in order to destroy the German forces.

On D-Day itself, five thousand Allied fighters filled the sky and swept away the one hundred and nineteen German fighters which opposed them. With the air superiority of fifty to one, rocket-firing Typhoons of the Allied air force had a field day, combing the terrain behind the Normandy beaches for any sign of movement on the ground. By mid-day on June 6th 1944, Allied fighters were completely unopposed and in many instances the pilots could no

The tremendous advantage gained by the Allies with their foresight in providing the Mulberry harbours was one of the keys to victory in Normandy.

The aftermath of RAF attack on German transport equipment at Rouen, August 1944.

longer find a target. In some cases, there was competition between the Allied fighters to attack the German vehicles which were foolhardy enough to venture onto the roads.

For a normal day in the Battle of Normandy, not even for a big operation or a special battle, the Allies would have on call an average of three thousand tactical sorties per day, as opposed to three hundred for the Germans; a ten to one superiority in the air, as a matter of course. In the case of a special attack, that number could increase by a vast amount. This naturally affected the whole conduct of the battle. It meant that German reinforcements were slow getting to Normandy because they had been delayed and took casualties on the route before they ever got into action. It meant that once they were in action they were pinned in place because every time they tried to manoeuvre, Allied aircraft attacked them.

Newsreels of the period show German vehicles covered in branches in an attempt to disguise any vehicle movements from the air. The crews constantly scanned the horizon for the first signs of the British fighter bombers which made any movement on the ground an extremely hazardous undertaking.

After the war, Fritz Bayerlein and the commander of the Panzer Lehr Division recorded the effects of the Allied air attacks. General Bayerlein, like all the other divisional commanders on the ground, knew that in the face of Allied air superiority it was almost suicidal to move during the day. Nonetheless, in their desire to rush as many troops into battle as quickly as possible, the German High Command proved to be stubbornly inflexible, as Bayerlein bitterly recalled.

"At 2 o'clock in the morning of 6th June I was alerted that the invasion fleet was coming across the Channel. I was told to begin moving north that afternoon at 5 o'clock. Well this was too early. Air attacks had been severe in the daylight and everyone knew that everything that could fly would support the invasion. My request for a delay until twilight was refused. So we moved as ordered and

In addition to their aerial advantage, the Allied armies were lavishly equipped with artillery and ammunition. The German forces had to be careful to conserve their ammunition and they could not, therefore, take part in the heavy counter-battery firing which was a speciality of the British artillery.

immediately came under Allied air attack. I lost twenty or thirty vehicles by nightfall. At daylight next morning, the commander of the 7th Army, gave me a direct order to proceed and there was nothing else I could do so the vehicles moved off as ordered.

By the end of the day I had lost forty trucks and ninety others. Five of my tanks were knocked out and eighty-four half tracks, prime movers and self-propelled guns. These were serious losses for a division not yet in action".

- CHAPTER 7 -
HOBART'S FUNNIES

The planning for D-Day progressed carefully throughout 1943 and it is a tribute to effective planning that some innovative technology was developed which would make a vital contribution to D-Day.

Despite the adverse experience at Dieppe, the sturdy hull of the Churchill tank was chosen as the basis for a highly versatile range of specialist machines known by the initials AVRE, which stood for Assault Vehicle Royal Engineers. They were formed into a special command of the 79th Armoured Division under Major-General P.C.S. Hobart.

As a direct result of the experience gained in the Dieppe raid, an ingenious variety of AVRE's were designed to assist in the real attack on Hitler's Atlantic Wall. The most important of these was a special adaptation of the Churchill which had its main gun replaced by a massive 290mm mortar known as a petard. This device could hurl a huge explosive charge known to the troops as 'the flying dustbin', which was intended to blow apart concrete defences of the type which had proved so effective against the tanks at Dieppe.

In a throwback to the days of World War One, the hull of the AVRE was also found to be capable of carrying a bundle of wood, eight feet in diameter, known as a fascine. This unlikely cargo could be dropped into an anti-tank ditch to create a simple bridge to allow tanks to cross.

For crossing larger obstacles such as sea walls, the AVRE could also be adapted to carry a box girder bridge with a span of thirty feet, which was capable of carrying vehicles up to forty tonnes in weight. In the event that the soft sand of the beaches would prove too difficult for tanks to cross, yet another variation on the the AVRE was developed. This one carried what was known as a 'bobbin',

The Churchill 'Crocodile' went into action a few minutes after the landing in Normandy in June 1944.

a huge reel of canvas which was a unrolled in front of the tank to allow the vehicle to cross areas of soft sand.

In order to prevent exploding mines making huge craters in the soft sand of the beach, there was also a variant of the AVRE which carried a huge plough on the front of the tank, designed to bring mines to the surface so that they could be detonated later on.

Finally in the list of specialist machines, which had become affectionately known to the troops as 'Hobart's funnies', was a demolition version of the AVRE which was capable of lumbering up to concrete defences and attaching a massive demolition charge against pillboxes and other obstructions before cautiously backing away and firing the charge.

While the specialist machines were at work on their particular tasks, they still needed the support of conventional armour, to protect them against anti-tank guns or enemy tanks . For that purpose, the Allies relied on two main variants of the trusty Sherman tank. The first of these was the Duplex drive, or DD swimming tank. This used a collapsible canvas screen and a propeller mounted on the back of the tank to allow the vehicle to swim ashore and reach the shallow water where they could neutralise enemy anti-tank positions while the specialist tanks went about their work of breaching the enemy defences.

One of the main elements of Rommel's defensive strategy lay in a massive belt of anti-tank mines along the entire length of the coast which in places stretched to a depth of half a mile from the shoreline. This first line was intended to be backed up by an additional belt of mines up to five miles deep sited further inland. It has been calculated that this grandiose scheme would have required two hundred million mines to complete. Despite the more limited resources available to him, Rommel still boasted that the beaches would become what he described as "a zone of death".

Although the Atlantic Wall was still far from complete, in mid-1944 the defences were fairly well advanced in the Normandy area. A considerable effort on the Allied side went into the development of vehicles which could be used to clear a path through the minefields. One such vehicle was the second main variant of the Sherman tank

The Churchill AVRE.

M4 SHERMAN CRAB
MINE-CLEARING FLAIL

Based on an original idea by a South African, Major A.S. du Toit, the Sherman Crab sported twin booms which projected from the front of the tank. These enormous whirling flails exploded and cleared mines in the tanks' path. The flails could be lifted in order to operate the vehicle as a conventional tank.

known as the Crab. It was a flail tank, which carried a mechanical device designed to beat the area in front of the tank, using steel chains which would explode any mines in the path of the vehicle.

With this mind-boggling collection of the specialist vehicles at his disposal, Hobart's 79th Division resembled a contractor's yard with a specialist machine for almost every conceivable application. The British and Canadian forces operating on D-Day, possibly with the experience of Dieppe still in mind, took full advantage of Hobart

A flail-tank goes ahead. First used in the great breakthrough at El Alamein, flail-tanks had a steel cylinder in front, to which lengths of chain were attached and which rotated rapidly as the tank moved forward.

and his 'funnies' as the vehicles were affectionately known. The American General Bradley, however, is alleged to have declined all offers of assistance, and this was to have disastrous consequences for the American forces fighting on Omaha Beach. In practice there may have been a less controversial explanation.

More than fifty years on, David Fletcher of the Royal Tank Museum offers a more sanguine explanation:

"The old argument runs that we didn't invent it, therefore it can't be any good. At least that's the one that is usually put forward. I think if we look at the 79th Armoured Division the truth is that it simply wasn't big enough to serve three armies. It was already serving the British and Canadian armies. I think if we'd extended it to support the Americans, except in very special cases, we would have been spread too thin. As to why the Americans did not adopt specialised armour themselves, the Churchill, which was the basis for most of the AVREs, would have been an anachronism to them. It was so different to anything they produced that they would never have got used to it. The Churchill was a dreadful tank by American standards. They did, however, adopt flails later in the campaign."

CHURCHILL ASSAULT VEHICLE ROYAL ENGINEERS (AVRE)

AVRE 290mm Petard Mortar and its ammunition.

The effectiveness of the concrete defences at Dieppe underlined the need for an infantry support tank which could overcome the toughest beach defences. Produced as a weapon to combat armoured strongpoints, the Churchill AVRE carried a 9-inch mortar which fired a 40lb 'dustbin' charge up to a range of 230 yards.

The Churchill 'Crocodile' could throw flames over 150 yards, either in rapid succession with fifty yard long 'gouts' or in a single continuous stream.

Of fifty Crabs and one hundred and twenty-eight AVRES deployed on D-Day, twelve Crabs were knocked out and twenty-two of the AVRES, a mercifully small sacrifice for so much progress. Harold Pitts of the Royal Marines, later recalled the experience of landing the DD tanks.

"Our job was to launch the floating tanks. It was very doubtful we should get them in because it was so rough but fortunately the landing was about half past five in the morning. Fortunately, it went very calm; for a clear spell, we were able to do what we wanted. It went on from there, Nelson was covering and several other ships. We got a little shot at the start but we got away with it. We operated on there for quite some time then slipped over into Gold Beach. Finally we lost all our ships. We came back to England to re-equip up to go again".

- CHAPTER 8 -
D-DAY

In the month of May 1944, Rear Admiral George Elvey Creasy, of the Royal Navy, Chief of Staff to Admiral Sir Bertram Ramsay, the Commander of the Allied Naval Expeditionary Force, concluded an address to Allied naval officers with these words: *"Gentlemen, what Philip of Spain failed to do, what Napoleon tried and failed to do and what Hitler never had the courage to try, we are about to do, and with God's grace we shall."* For many days before those words were spoken, an immense and intricate machine had been in motion.

The assault forces were gathered at countless points of embarkation along the southern shores of England; British and Canadians for the most part to the east, Americans to the west. The final stages of this initial movement saw an important link-up between the disposition of ships and landing craft and the drafting of army units into the special marshalling areas near the coast.

To embark assault forces, a different technique was required from that used for simply transporting units overseas. It was essential for the assault that, as far as possible, the first wave of troops should go in as self- supporting combat teams. It was also necessary that the support units should be well spread among the hundreds of ships, so that any casualties inflicted by German air action would not unduly affect any particular aspect of the assault.

This important function of 'breaking up' led to the movement staffs in the marshalling areas gaining the nick-name 'mincing machines.' As units passed from the marshalling camps they lost their identity and became serially numbered components of craft and ship loads. So, from the 'hards' and quays, infantrymen, artillerymen, sappers and all the others who went to make up the 1944 army, boarded the invasion ships and became part of a team that could fight its way up from the beaches.

The roads of southern England, hastily prepared less than four years earlier to meet a potential invader, were thronged with tanks, guns, bulldozers, lorries and 'DUKWs', the amphibious vehicles first used in Sicily.

"I was in the Normandy landings on D-Day. I was attached to the 3rd Canadian Division and we were landing the troops, the Canadians, on the beaches. I was what you called a 'Duck' driver. Most people know its abbreviated name DUKW's. For the life of me, I still can't remember what it meant."

For miles inland, these assorted vehicles lined the way in almost unbroken chains, while vapour trails high in the summer skies marked the path of the fighter aircraft.

The RAF, with the US air forces, had brought about a complete transformation since the dog-fighting days of the Battle of Britain. Both the armies and the mass of shipping that was to transport them, could gather with little fear of major interference from the Luftwaffe. Indeed, as was to be proved beyond doubt in a few

An aerial view of the thousands of ships gathered together to support the Normandy landings gives an impression of the overwhelming logistical advantages which lay with the Allies.

M4 SHERMAN DD (DUPLEX DRIVE) SWIMMING TANK

DD Sherman tank with its flotation screen lowered

The M4 Sherman DD played a major role in the D-Day landings in June 1944. It was supported by a collapsible canvas screen which was lowered when the tank hit the beach. The waterproofed DD was a successful British adaptation of an American weapon.

The DD Tanks in the first wave were soon supported by other Shermans landed by more conventional means.

days, the once much-vaunted German airforce was now not even capable of carrying out the reconnaissance that would have given the Germans warning of the time and direction of our attack.

The soldiers embarking in the ships were in great heart. On June 1st, everything was ready, and Admiral Ramsay issued this memorable 'Order of the Day' to the Allied Naval forces:

"It is to be our privilege to take part in the greatest amphibious operation in history, a necessary preliminary to the opening of the Western Front in Europe which, in conjunction with the great Russian advance, will crush the fighting power of Germany. This is the opportunity which we have long awaited and which must be seized and pursued with relentless determination; the hopes and prayers of the free world and of the enslaved peoples of Europe will be with us, and we cannot fail them. Our task, in conjunction with the Merchant Navies of the United Nations and supported by the Allied Air Forces, is to carry the Allied Expeditionary Force to the Continent, to establish there a secure bridge-head, and to build it up and maintain it at a rate which will outmatch that of the enemy. Let no one underestimate the magnitude of this task. The Germans are desperate, and will resist fiercely until we out-manoeuvre and out-fight them, which we can and we will do. To every one of you will

American troops crowd into their landing craft prior to June 6th. One can imagine the discomfort of the men when the operation, originally scheduled for June 5th, was postponed for another 24 hours leaving them cramped in claustrophobic conditions.

US G.I.s on board their landing craft en-route to the Normandy beaches. Those who were fortunate enough to land on Utah beach had a much easier time than the forces destined for Omaha.

be given the opportunity to show by his determination and resource that dauntless spirit of resolution which individually strengthens and inspires and which collectively is irresistible. I count on every man to do his utmost to ensure the success of this great enterprise, which is the climax of the European war. Good luck to you all and Godspeed."

The secret of the point of assault was well kept. Many commanders did not know where their men would go in, until they had been embarked and "sealed" in landing craft. Only then could the disclosure could be made, and there was a scramble to study a map of the Bay of the Seine.

THE ALLIED PLAN

The British, including the Canadians, were going in on the eastern beaches, with the Caen canal on their left flank and covered by airborne troops dropped a few hours earlier on the other side of the canal, while the Americans attacked to the west, where the broad bay sweeps round towards Cherbourg.

The vital sea lift was to be undertaken by two main forces - the Eastern Force under the command of Rear Admiral Sir Philip Vian, of the Royal Navy, and the Western Force under the command of Rear Admiral Alan G. Kirk, of the United States Navy. The Eastern Force consisted of three naval assault forces and one follow-up force, and the Western of two naval assault forces and one follow-up force. The warships and larger vessels involved were eighty per cent British, but the overall percentage, which took in many smaller craft, was sixty per cent British and forty per cent American. The total number of vessels taking part in the assault was given by Admiral Ramsay as five thousand, one hundred and forty-three.

Allied troops come ashore on Fortress Europe. The soldier in the foreground with his spectacles and slight figure produces a less than convincing picture of the rugged hero.

OPERATION OVERLORD

Even today, Operation Overlord still ranks as the largest and most complex single military operation ever staged. In many respects, the Allies could consider themselves fortunate. Although their full objectives were not achieved, in every case they managed to get significant forces ashore and in most instances had achieved penetrations of approximately five miles in depth. In the first wave there were 57,000 American troops and more than 75,000 Canadian and British troops, plus their supporting armour, artillery and engineers, who were to assault the beaches of the Normandy resorts in France. The codenames of those beaches have become beacons in military history: Utah, Omaha, Gold, Juno and Sword.

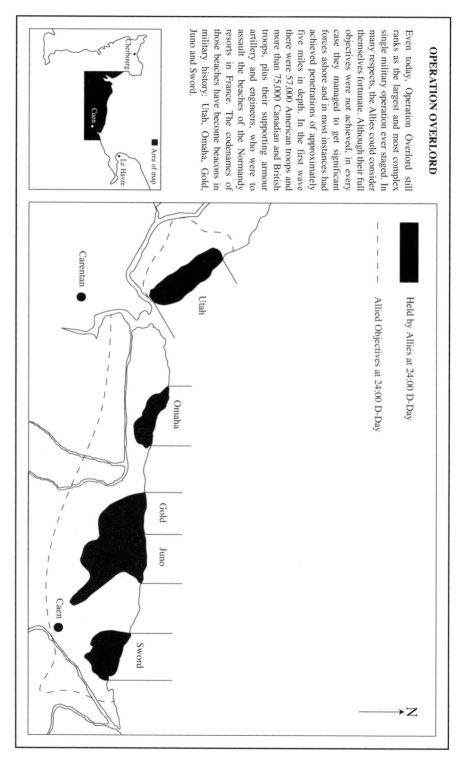

■ Held by Allies at 24:00 D-Day

– – – Allied Objectives at 24:00 D-Day

N →

158

CHOOSING THE DAY

The Momentous decision of which day to choose for D-Day rested on the shoulders of the Supreme Allied Commander, General Dwight D. Eisenhower. He originally selected D-Day as the 5th of June, being the day when the tides best suited the invasion. But as early as June 1st the pattern of the weather, which until then had been fine and sunny, suddenly changed. Heavy rains now appeared, which both reduced visibility in the channel and also produced very heavy seas.

On June 1st, when the first meeting to discuss the weather forecast for D-Day was held, the outlook was not good, and it deteriorated during the next three days.

No single topic was more anxiously debated in the planning of the operation than the date and hour at which the invasion was to take place. The appropriate choice depended on conditions of tide, conditions of light, the possibility of postponement for bad weather

Looking for all the world as if they were on a peacetime day trip, German prisoners await the transport which would ship them back to England and captivity.

This picture taken on June 7th provides a vivid impression of the huge scale of the undertaking which was operation Neptune.

and a host of other considerations, all of which were most carefully weighed. The date finally chosen was June 5th, with the 6th and 7th as possible alternatives. No one, however, expected the decision to be as difficult as it actually was. In London, the weekend before D-Day, was overcast with low scudding clouds and squalls of wind. On the evening of June 3rd, however, the Supreme Commander decided to allow the forces to move, despite the unfavourable outlook, in order to gain the advantage of launching the operation on the first possible day.

Eisenhower and his senior commanders met to consider the situation. It is not too difficult to imagine the tension that there must have been at the meeting, where the Allied commanders pondered the decision whether to allow the invasion to go ahead on the 5th or ask for a cancellation. The pattern of tides meant that really only a twenty-four hour delay was possible, otherwise the entire operation would have to be cancelled for another two weeks. Finally at 4.15am, after much deliberation, the order was given to postpone the invasion until June 6th. This meant that many of the troops already packed into the landing craft faced another uncomfortable day and night waiting in the cramped confines of their craft. Sea sickness was rife and by the time the real order came many of the men were dispirited, tired and on the verge of mutiny. As for the craft, the huge fleet needed at least twenty-four hours notice to ensure that the co-ordination necessary for such an undertaking could be organised. A second meeting was called for 9.30pm on the evening of June 4th. Despite the unpromising look of the weather the official meteorologist RAF Captain James Stagg gave the commanders a slight ray of hope. Weather ships stationed in the channel had indicated that there might just be a brief period of clearer weather and calm seas early on the morning of June 6th. The decision was now down to one man; Eisenhower. The

Infantrymen taking cover from enemy snipers behind a M.10 tank destroyer.

HANDBOOK ON GERMAN MILITARY FORCES
EXTRACT NO.11
BATTLE GROUPS
IN DELAYING ACTION

"....Battle groups normally are organised for the execution of some specific task in the withdrawal, such as a local counterattack or the defence of some particular feature whose retention is necessary for the security of the main withdrawal.

Battle groups, which the Germans employ for offensive and defensive as well as delaying missions, vary in size from a company or two, with attached close support weapons, to a regiment or several battalions reinforced with tanks, artillery, antiaircraft, engineer, and reconnaissance elements. In all cases the Germans seek to make them as self-sufficient as possible in combat. In actual practice, however, the composition of German battle groups appears often to have been dictated less by the theory of what units should be put together to form a self-sufficient combat force, than by the demands of an emergency situation which commanders have been forced to meet with the insufficient and normally disassociated units at their disposal.

German battle groups may be organised for short, long, or changing missions. They are usually known by the name of their commander.

To prevent the pursuing enemy columns from approaching close enough to engage even their rear guard elements, the Germans continually employ demolitions and obstacles of all kinds. The thoroughness with which engineer operations have been carried out has increased steadily throughout the war. Culverts and bridges are completely destroyed. Roads and all natural detours are mined, cratered, or blocked by felled trees; in streets and villages, streets are blocked by the wreckage of buildings. Vertical rail obstacles are placed to obstruct main routes; mines often are laid for thirty yards around the edge of the obstacle. Wooden box mines are used to a large extent as demolition charges, and aerial bombs and artillery shells are sometimes similarly employed.

Frequently rear parties are committed to a delaying engagement in order to cover the preparation of demolitions immediately behind them. During static periods in the general withdrawal,when the Germans occupy their line of resistance or phase line, engineer units prepare demolitions in the rear. After the withdrawal, these demolitions are covered by sniper fire, machine guns, and self-propelled weapons as long as possible...."

Nebelwerfer rockets launched from a specially converted half track proved to be an extremely potent weapon which could be quickly moved to a new position after firing.

163

air chiefs were unconvinced that the 6th was a good day to allow them to offer effective air cover. Naturally they needed a day with the assurance of good visibility. The Navy however was confident that the seas in the summer season would be easily navigable even in bad weather. Of the Army chiefs, Montgomery in particular was the most enthusiastic. *"I would say - go,"* was Montgomery's famous quote. It is recorded that Eisenhower sat for a long time in a period of nervous silence before he made the statement: *"I am quite positive that we must give the order, I don't like it but there it is."* In order to give themselves one last opportunity to reverse the decision, a subsequent meeting was called for 4am on June 5th. Once again, however, the reports were reasonably good and Eisenhower finally committed the Allies irrevocably to the assault on June 6th, with the legendary phrase, *"OK, let's go."* A.V. Alexander, first Lord of the Admiralty recalled the tension of those days in a speech to the House of Commons on March 7th, 1945:

"On the morning of June 5th, the forecast stated that developments overnight showed slight improvement in the general situation, which appeared at that moment more favourable. On the strength of this forecast, the irrevocable decision to make the assault in the early hours of June 6th was taken. The decision was a terribly hard one. Events leave no doubt that it was right. Had the opportunity been missed, the operation could not have taken place for another fortnight, and by then the weather was even worse. In its combination of high winds and cloud, June 1944 was the worst June for fifty years. Nevertheless, it seems likely that the wildness of the weather may have led the Germans to believe that we could not launch the assault, and it may therefore have contributed to their apparent unreadiness, and to the astonishing success of the assault."

Nobody had been surprised when news came that a postponement of twenty-four hours had been decided upon on June 4th. Tides on the other side of the Channel were all important, however, and the expedition had to be undertaken on the 5th, 6th or 7th. The wind was still blowing strongly next morning, June 5th, but once again the little ships, recalled the previous night, began to leave the anchorage. This time it was no false start:

"We were moved then down to Southampton and put on board an infantry landing craft. We put out to sea and we went round and round in circles for about three or four days, in and out, in and out, nobody wanted to stay aboard because the sea was that rough, you didn't float - you flew on them. We came back eventually to Portsmouth for re-fuelling, and then we did go across on the Normandy D-Day."

Up and down the coast, shipping was on the move, with the minesweeping forces in the van. They consisted of three hundred and nine British, twenty-two American and sixteen Canadian minesweepers. Having concluded preliminary sweeps, they now had to open broad highways of more than thirty miles in length which ended only when they could get no closer to the Normandy beaches. They were followed by special vessels known as 'danners',

American wounded at a beach dressing station waiting to be transported to England by sea.

British troops take up a defensive position in the ruins of Caen. The man in the foreground has his bayonet fixed, although in this type of terrain hand-to-hand fighting was unlikely to occur.

which laid 'danbuoys' (to indicate dangerous areas) along the swept thoroughfares. Despite the dangers, the troops were delighted to be finally ashore.

Harvey Pearman recalls the uncertainty which surrounded the decision to go:

"I landed on Juno beach, and they put us on the boats a couple of days before, then they postponed the landings. We were rolling about on these landing craft for a couple of days before they decided to take off because of the weather. When we got out in the Channel there were minesweepers on each side of us, escorting us over to Normandy. I think we were on the landing craft nearly twenty-four hours on the crossing, which is about a hundred miles across to Normandy from Southampton, and I wondered where we were going. I remember being in the top of this LST. We went all through the night in this LST, I was right in the top more or less, and you could hear it creaking away there, you just didn't even know where you were going."

For the seaborne forces, 'H-Hour' in the eastern sector was fixed at 7.25am on June 6th, the US forces in the western sector going in fifty minutes earlier. Airborne landings were made several hours before that in the vicinity of the east bank of the Caen Canal, and, astride the Cherbourg peninsula. Dropping by parachute or going in in gliders, these crack British and American troops secured important communication points and covered the flanks of the assault forces.

The extreme left and right flanks of the invasion front were to be protected by British 6th Airborne Division's parachute drops in the area to the East of Caen, and by the American 101st Airborne Division, who would be dropped in the immediate area of Carentan. Both of these drops were to proceed the landings themselves. On the British flank the drop met with considerable success; glider-borne troops were able to assist in the capture of the famous Pegasus bridge over the Caen canal. They also captured a very menacing German battery situated in Merville, directly overlooking Sword beach.

THE AIRFORCES INTERVENE

As darkness fell on June 5th over the heavy seas which tossed the flat bottomed assault craft like so many corks, RAF aircraft were preparing to take off for the opening round of the battle of the beaches.

In the early hours of the morning the drone of their engines could be heard above the whistle of the wind in the rigging of the ships. About seven hundred and fifty heavy bombers, guided by Pathfinders, carried out a concentrated bombing designed to soften up the German positions in the coastal area. They carried on until two hours before H-Hour, and then the 'mediums' went over and dropped their deadly cargoes on previously pin-pointed coastal defence batteries.

As dawn broke on D-Day, the fires started by the heavy bombers acted like beacons for the incoming ships. The coast of France was clearly visible when the heaviest air blow of all was struck immediately before H-Hour. Fortresses and Liberators of the US 8th and 9th Air Forces, covered by an umbrella of fighters, unloaded two thousand four hundred tons of bombs on the British beaches and nineteen hundred tons on the American beaches. The complete absence of the Luftwaffe at this time must have been grimly suggestive to the stunned German defenders of things to come; that is, if they were still capable of appreciating the situation. All the same, until the Allies obtained their first landing strip in France, it was necessary to maintain ten fighter squadrons in the south of England in order that at least one should be continually over the beaches on the other side of the Channel.

The warships going in towards the coast seemed to be waiting for the guns of the Atlantic Wall to challenge them. Finally, as if they had despaired of the coming of the challenge, the bombarding ships

A German Grenadier equipped with the Panzerschrek or 'Stove Pipe'. This powerful anti-tank weapon was highly efficient at short range.

A German machine gunner in the ruins of Caen. These ruins provided the ideal offensive position for the experienced German troops, many of whom had seen action in the terrible Russian campaign.

opened up. Huge yellow flashes and big mushrooms of brownish cordite fumes split the horizon and a few seconds later, the deep rumble that was to grow into a continuous roar, came from the Allied fleet. With little more than forty minutes to go to H-Hour, British 'Hunt' class destroyers raced in to engage in close duels with any surviving shore batteries. American destroyers, to the west, were similarly at work, and the heavier guns of the battleships had taken up the onslaught and were hurling fourteen, fifteen and sixteen inch shells across the beaches.

The final close-up punch before the assault troops poured ashore, was delivered by rocket firing craft.

The rockets cascaded on what remained of the German forward positions, and the vessels that fired them momentarily disappeared behind a sheet of flame from the rockets.

"To the minesweepers fell the dangerous task of leading the

assault forces to the beaches. The sweeping of ten approach channels was the largest single minesweeping operation ever undertaken in war. Three hundred and nine British, sixteen Canadian, and twenty-two US minesweepers took part. The minesweepers then had to widen all the approach channels and to sweep areas off the beaches for the reception of the vast numbers of ships needed to keep the Army supplied.... The operation was the greatest single achievement of a never ending labour, in which over fifteen thousand mines had to be swept.

The next forces to go into action were the bombardment ships. These forces took part in the drenching of the beach defences, immediately before the assault. As one of the bombarding forces arrived in position at 5.15am, four enemy E-boats and some armed trawlers from Le Havre made a half-hearted attack, and sank one Norwegian destroyer by torpedo. Our forces sank an enemy trawler, and damaged another, and the attack was not renewed.

Then came the moment for which the whole world had waited; the moment when Allied Forces again set foot on the soil of France. The outstanding fact of the day was that, despite the unfavourable weather, the Naval operations were carried out in every important respect as planned. Tactical surprise, which had not been expected, was achieved. Losses of ships and landing craft of all types were much lower than had been expected."

H-HOUR

Then, as H-Hour arrived, there was a 'silence' which, by comparison, was as impressive as the roar of the guns. In that lull the assault craft made the final run and bumped on to the beach. The tide was low, so that many of the enemy obstacles were exposed to view, but some of the assault craft were caught by angle irons and, with bottoms ripped open, were sinking as they made the French shore. Still, the crews of the little craft had the grim satisfaction of knowing that they had put their passengers ashore. Mines were touched off, but men thrown into the sea scrambled ashore and went forward with the rest. It is recorded that sailors from these vessels were so much with the troops, that they left their craft and ran up the beaches in order to wish a final 'good luck' to the soldiers.

THE DD TANKS

On D-Day itself, the experience of the DD swimming tanks varied massively from beach to beach. Of the thirty tanks which attacked Utah beach, twenty-nine made it safely to the shore, where they played a major role in supporting the infantry in their drive inland. At Omaha Beach, however, where sea conditions were much rougher, in the first battalion twenty-eight out of thirty DD tanks sank to the ocean floor, many taking their crews with them. Initially deprived of armour support, casualties among the American infantry on Omaha were the highest of D-Day.

The commander of the second battalion, seeing the sea conditions refused to launch his tanks and demanded instead that his landing craft deposit them directly onto the beach. This was successfully done but valuable time was lost.

On the Canadian Juno Beach, the situation was more positive, and twenty-one out of thirty-four DD tanks made it to the shore. Overall, the British had better luck than either the Canadians or the Americans, and thirty-one out of thirty-four DD tanks launched at Sword Beach made it to the shore.

On Juno Beach, the DD tanks were particularly effective in assisting the Canadian infantry, who had been pinned down by some well prepared German defences. The arrival of the swimming tanks soon neutralised the German anti-tank guns and allowed the advance to continue inland. Also on Juno Beach, the AVRE machines proved that they too could be highly effective. Not only did they successfully clear the beach of mines, but using their

An injured British soldier is brought back to England from the Normandy beaches on D-Day. It was a feature of the effectiveness of the Allied planning, that the first wounded actually arrived back in England on D-Day itself, when this picture was taken.

petards, they were able to breach the sea wall and drop fascines into the anti-tank ditch, which allowed the supporting infantry to attack German strong points in the houses behind the beach. Here too, they played a vital role and they were able to offer assistance to the infantry by demolishing German strong points.

Inevitably, some pockets of Germans escaped the amazing bombardment because many of the concrete pillboxes went deep underground. Even sentries were provided with concrete reinforced holes in the ground, over which they could pull heavy concrete lids. At many points, therefore, the dash across the sands had to be made in the face of rifle and machine-gun fire.

At Bernieres, a single German gun held its fire until about a dozen craft were on the beach in point blank range. Its courageous crew then opened fire and caused a number of casualties before they were wiped out by a rain of shells from the ships.

BLOODY OMAHA

The hardest fighting on the whole length of the beaches came in the American sector and on Omaha beach in particular. By one of the few strokes of misfortune that befell the Allies on that fateful day, the Americans found themselves confronted by strong and determined German forces. The explanation came later; the Germans had chosen the very time of the assault in that particular zone as the time for an anti-invasion training exercise, so resistance was greater than expected.

It was obvious to ships lying off-shore that some very hard fighting was going on, and that the Americans were finding it very difficult to get a foothold. Disregarding the risk they themselves ran, the ships, including some Canadian minesweepers, got in as close as they possibly could and gave close gun support to the Americans.

The US parachute drop was also less fortunate than their British counterparts. Rommel had ordered that any likely drop areas in the immediate vicinity of Carentan were to be flooded. In addition they were heavily sown with anti-personnel mines which caused heavy casualties.

The German 7th Army came under the command of General Dolmann, but he himself was absent from the invasion area on June 6th. On Utah beach the Americans enjoyed considerably more success, although ironically it started with what was potentially the seeds of a failure. As the hundreds of craft made for the shore hidden by a smoke screen, they were intended to be shepherded by patrol craft PC1176, which would guide them to the appropriate beach. Unfortunately, the patrol craft hit a mine and was completely destroyed. As the other craft carried on to the shore they drifted into an off-shore current and were carried down stream, two kilometres too far to the south. Increasingly, this actually turned out to be a

Bayeux, the ancient city of Normandy, was taken undamaged on June 7th, 1944. The liberating Allied troops received a frantic reception from the people crowding the streets with tears streaming down their cheeks.

blessing in disguise, as once ashore, Brigadier General Theodore Roosevelt Junior, the son of the president, soon realised that the beach that he had landed on was far less defended than the beach which had originally been assigned to them. Roosevelt urged the troops to move as quickly as possible inshore, to overcome the light German defences. As he walked with the aid of a stick, Roosevelt had to fight hard to be allowed to go ashore, and in fact was the only American Allied General to do so. His heroism on D-Day, however, was to be almost his last act. Tragically, Roosevelt died of a heart attack on June 12th, but he was awarded a posthumous medal of honour for his conspicuous bravery on D-Day.

THE CANADIANS ATTACK

The main Canadian attack was on a ten thousand yard front in the region of Courseulles and Bernieres. The sappers, working right in the front of the assault, as they did all along the line, cleared the dangerous obstructions, often with the aid of bulldozers, and the infantry went through four main gaps. On their own sectors, the work of the Royal Engineers and American sappers was not finished when they had made the first safe paths through the extreme seaward defences. They continued to enlarge the openings, and days later were still making the beach areas safe for the great build-up.

Men of the Essex Scottish Regiment, who had seen action in the Dieppe raid, and the Fusiliers Mont Royal were among the first of the Canadians to storm across the beaches. A battalion of the Royal Berkshire Regiment went in with the Canadians. Many other English county regiments were strongly represented as the Allied flood broke upon the Normandy shore. The Royal Warwickshires, the King's Own Yorkshire Light Infantry, the South Lancashires, the Durham Light Infantry and the Cheshires, were among the first of the regiments that added the assault on Normandy to their battle honours.

Commanded by Major-General R.F.L. Keller, C.B.E., the 3rd Canadian Infantry Division seen here was among the first units to go ashore in Normandy on June 6th, 1944.

There was a place of honour in the forefront of the attack for the 3rd British Infantry Division. This was the same division which had been led by Major General Montgomery, as he then was, in France in 1940 during the disastrous fall of France. They were now back at the landings on June 6th 1944, commanded by Major General T.G. Rennie.

The British 50th Division in particular was engaged in some hard fighting, but swept on to its objectives and well earned the praise of the Commander of the Corps to which it belonged: *"Well done, indeed, 50th Division. Champion!"*

The 59th Infantry Division was another British division early ashore. The 4th/7th Dragoon Guards were among the first armoured troops to land, and later led the advance towards Villers-Bocage and assisted in the capture of Tilly. The 13th/18th Hussars, another armoured formation, landed at Colleville-sur-Orne.

A battalion of the King's Royal Rifle Corps was one of the first British units to land in France; the Rifle Brigade and the Royal Ulster Rifles were also among the first ashore. The King's Own Scottish Borderers took part in the storming of the Atlantic Wall, but the full weight of the famous 51st Highland Division was to be felt by the Germans only in the days that followed, when the whole success of the campaign was ensured by the destruction of the main German forces in the fierce battles that raged around Caen. The Black Watch, the Gordons and the Seaforths, the last particularly at St Honorine la Chardonnerette, would carve out another famous chapter in Normandy.

Wales, the West Country and London the 4th County of London Yeomanry, (the Sharpshooters), were also represented on that great day.

THE NAVAL DIMENSION

The Naval forces required for the assault landing consisted of four main classes: minesweepers, to clear the way for all the ships and craft which would follow; landing craft and ships of all kinds to carry the soldiers and the guns, tanks, transport and other equipment with which they would fight; bombarding ships, whose task, with the Air Force, would be to destroy German opposition to the landing, and enable the Army to gain the lodgement which it required before it could deploy its own weapons; finally there were escort and anti-submarine forces.

Besides the battleships, twenty-two cruisers and many more destroyers joined in the bombardment, which was to continue as long as German forces remained within range. Among the famous ships that played a prominent part were the British cruisers 'Apollo', 'Argonaut', 'Belfast', 'Bellona', 'Black Prince', 'Ceres', 'Danae', 'Arethusa', 'Diadem', 'Enterprise', 'Frobisher', 'Glasgow', 'Hawkins', 'Mauritius', 'Orion', and 'Scylla', and the American cruisers 'Tuscaloosa', 'Augusta' and 'Quincy', and the Polish cruiser 'Dragon'. In the course of the bombardment, 56,769 shells of 4.7inch or greater calibre were fired.

The naval guns not only offered continual support to the Allied troops but frequently intervened at specific points where the heavy weight of their concentrated fire carried the day in Allied favour.

177

American soldiers dragged ashore by their colleagues in the wake of the destruction of their landing craft. The heavy weight of the equipment carried by men on the D-Day landings caused many of those who did fall into the sea to drown, so these men are lucky to reach the shore.

HMS Rodney and HMS Ramillies, for instance, were called upon to put down a heavy fire on German forces from the 21st Panzer Division who were attempting to split the British and Americans. The German effort failed, thanks largely to the work of the great naval guns. For a time the troops on the eastern end of the assault beaches were troubled by enemy artillery fire coming from the other side of the Caen canal. British cruisers attacked these batteries and their fire was soon stopped.

THE AIR FORCES

The Allied air forces, too, continued to strike hard at the German forces. During the morning of D-Day more than thirteen hundred Liberators and Fortresses, with a large escort of fighters, bombed the Germans for two and a half hours without a break. The Luftwaffe scarcely appeared. One of the most massive attacks came at dusk a few evenings later. A vast fleet of bombers that filled the sky, flew over the long anchorage and devastated E- boats and other German concentrations in Le Havre.

The Luftwaffe did attempt to attack the shipping in the anchorage by bombing on the night of D-Day. The attack was not heavy and chiefly served to demonstrate the impressive number of anti-aircraft guns assembled in the ships and on the beaches. The whole anchorage seemed to be under a canopy of vivid tracer shells, while smoke made by the ships added to the confusion of the German airmen.

The situation for the German forces on June 6th was obviously complicated by their cumbersome and labyrinthine command process, but there were also other factors to take into account. The chronic lack of fuel severely curtailed the ability of reinforcements to move into the bridgehead area. But first, clear and concise orders

German prisoners under the guard of a British Tommy who looks particularly pleased with his haul. The Germans themselves had endured the massive aerial and naval bombardments and were probably very pleased to be out of the fighting.

had to be arranged and within the complex set-up that the German high command had, this was never going to be easy.

ROMMEL ABSENT

To further complicate matters, Rommel had chosen this precise time to go home on leave to visit his wife. As we have seen, Dolmann was also absent. The net effect of the confusion was that only the 21st Panzer Division was available to perform a counter-stroke against the Allies on June 6th.

The 21st Panzer Division was a famous name. It had served with great distinction in the Africa Korps under Rommel. That is not to say, however, that the men who were now under his command were veterans of the desert campaign. Very few German troops had survived the debacle in North Africa and the 21st Panzer Division was essentially a new formation with much less battle experience than the old desert formation. Nonetheless, they did perform their duty with reasonable skill. On June 6th, however, they were not available in sufficient numbers to achieve their objective which was to cut through the British Second Army and strike at the beachhead.

Sepp Deitrich, now in command of the 1st SS Panzer Corps, urgently fought to bring his formations into action. In addition to the Leibstandarte Division and the 12th SS Hitler Jugend Division, he was to assume control over the 21st Panzer Division. Allied interdiction meant that the SS forces arrived at the battle zone in a piecemeal fashion. In consequence, there was no concerted attempt to launch a serious counter-attack. The bulk of the British attacking forces in that sector fell upon the unfortunate 716th Infantry Division which had the job of defending the stretch of coast north of Caen.

Against all expectations, a battle group from the 21st Panzer Division did manage to exploit a gap between the British and Canadian forces and actually reached the coast at Lyon sur Mere at around 7 o'clock on the evening of 6th June. No reinforcements,

Another view of the US infantry leaving their landing craft bound for Utah beach.

however, were available and the German forces were forced to fall back to positions just north of Caen. The fighting on that day had cost the Division twenty-five per cent of its tanks and there was worse to follow.

Sepp Deitrich now arrived to take command of the immediate battle area. The 1st SS Panzer Corps now took the 21st Panzer Division and what little remained of the 716th Infantry Division under its command. As the Panzer Lehr Division was still making its way to the battle area and could not really be expected to be in action before the morning of June 8th, the 12th SS Panzer Division, Hitler Jugend had to make a strike against the 3rd Canadian Infantry Division to protect against an Allied thrust designed to capture Carpiquet aerodrome. This division was to see some intense fighting in the weeks that followed. On 7th June elements of the 21st Panzer Division and the 12th SS Panzer Division pressed home a heavy attack on the Canadians. The Canadian 9th Infantry Brigade was forced to withdraw and the Allies could make no further progress towards Caen.

Caen, of course, had been an objective for D-Day itself and at this stage no-one could possibly have suspected that it would take another six weeks before the town fell into Allied hands. In those brief actions the Canadians lost twenty-one Sherman tanks with seven more badly damaged. The 12th SS had lost nine Mark IV's with a few others damaged. On paper it looked as if the advantage was with the Germans, but the Allies could always replace their losses. It would be very difficult indeed for the 12th SS to replace the nine precious tanks which they had lost on only the second day of the battle.

During the morning of D-Plus One, (Wednesday, June 7th) General Montgomery arrived from England in HMS Faulknor. He

Dressed in his finest uniform, proudly displaying all of his decorations, SS General Sepp Dietrich enjoys a sunny morning over the newspapers. Dietrich was to play a crucial role in ensuring that the vital SS elements of the German armed forces in Normandy provided its customary role as the backbone in the defensive fighting.

A US infantryman, who was not fortunate enough to survive the attack on D-Day, lies where he fell on the sand.

paid a flying visit to the headquarters ship 'Hilary' before going ashore. In a final message to his troops he had wished them "Good hunting!" and now, asked how the hunting was going, he replied, "Very well - everything is going excellently."

Anxiety about the success of the assault had, in fact, ended. In many sectors, first, second and third objectives had been taken, and everything now depended on the rapid build-up behind the front line which, in some cases, was already six to eight miles from the coastal strip.

British Commandos and American Rangers had pulled off spectacular feats, and one Royal Marine Commando was even at that time covering itself with glory. They went in to capture Port en Bessin, a key point near the centre of the landings which was covered by three strong German defensive positions. It was intended that the Marines should land at Le Hamel, but as their craft went in they came under heavy fire from a German battery at Longues.

They had to swing off a mile to the east and, as they attempted to land there, five of their fourteen LCA's were mined and sank. The Marines from these swam ashore, salvaged what equipment they could and pushed inland with their comrades. Those who had lost theirs, re-armed themselves with weapons captured from the Germans and went on through Les Roquettes to La Rosiere, where they were met by heavy German mortar fire. They overcame this and silenced several machine-gun nests and then, despite the fact that every Marine carried a load of equipment and mortar ammunition, amounting to nearly three-quarters of a hundredweight, decided to save time by pushing across country.

They arrived in sight of their objective after covering ten miles, in time to see some of the preparatory work done by the Army, Navy and Air Force. The Germans in the little port were bombed from the air, shelled from the shore and also from the sea. Still, the Germans had heavily concreted positions and the opposition was fierce when the Marines went into the assault. As the fighting raged, the German garrison twice counter-attacked and won back the position, but the Marines came a third time and the garrison had had, by then, enough. When the Marine Commandos made contact with the Americans they linked the whole Allied front in Normandy.

CAEN HOLDS OUT

In heavy fighting with the 12th SS Hitler Jugend Division, it soon became apparent that the Germans were not going to give up Caen without a great fight. On the 8th June Montgomery wrote to the British Director of Military Operations: *The Germans are doing everything they can to hold onto Caen. I have decided not to have a lot of casualties by butting up against the place, so I have ordered 2nd Army to keep up good pressure at Caen and to make its main effort to Villers-Bocage.*

Villers-Bocage was a name which was to have an enduring reputation after the campaign. In particular it would be famous for the exploits of the 101st SS Heavy Panzer Battalion, but on 7th June that Battalion still had to begin its move from Bouvey and it was unlikely that there was much chance that, with a distance of at least two hundred and fifty kilometres to cover, they would reach the battle area before 9th June. In fact the first elements began to reach the battle zone on the 10th and, on the 11th June, in a battle between the SS Panther tanks and Canadian Shermans, thirty-four Shermans and three Fireflies were destroyed, for the loss of only two Panther tanks, with another severely damaged. This was yet another example of the qualitative advantage which the Germans enjoyed in terms of armour. The combination of numbers on the Allied side, however, along with air support and devastatingly accurate naval fire would help to swing the balance in favour of the Allies, but there was still a great deal of tough fighting to go.

The most desperate German resistance at this time was in the direction of Caen, where later the great battle of "the hinge" was to develop. Heroic work was being done on the left flank by the British airborne troops, who had struck with such swiftness that bridges, locks and canal installations were in their hands before the

German sentries could deploy the charges that would have blown these important military objectives sky-high.

At first, the reception given to Allied troops by the French was cool. But many people living in the coastal area of Normandy had had to face the shattering bombardment and bombing that destroyed so many German positions. Naturally they were dazed, shaken and angry. As a result, they first appeared apathetic, and for those who had suffered less, even hostile, but by D-Day Plus Two it was obvious that a new hope was springing up in them.

It became clear that this was not yet another raid which would be followed by Nazi retribution, but Liberation! With tears in their eyes they expressed their realisation of this, and flags of France, with the double cross of Lorraine added to the centre panel, began to appear everywhere.

Around Caen, a vitally important road junction in Normandy which marked the eastern bastion of the German defence positions, raged some of the fiercest fighting of the early days of the Allied invasion of France in 1944. The northern part was captured on July 9th, while the southern part was finally captured later on the 18th of July. By this time artillery and air bombardment had reduced it to ruins. This is the shell of the church of St Pierre as it looked in July 1944.

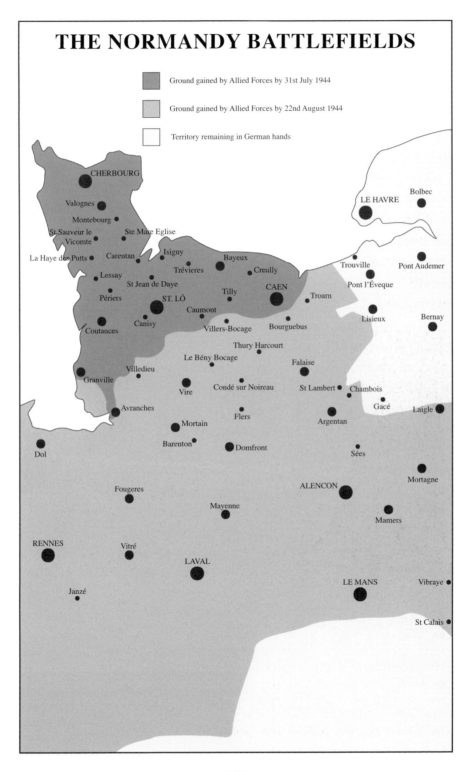

THE NORMANDY BATTLEFIELDS

Ground gained by Allied Forces by 31st July 1944

Ground gained by Allied Forces by 22nd August 1944

Territory remaining in German hands

CHERBOURG

Valognes

Montebourg

St Sauveur le Vicomte

Ste Mare Eglise

La Haye des Putts

Carentan

Isigny

Bayeux

LE HAVRE

Bolbec

Trévieres

Creully

Trouville

Pont Audemer

Lessay

St Jean de Daye

Tilly

CAEN

Pont l'Éveque

Périers

ST. LÔ

Troarn

Caumont

Lisieux

Bernay

Canisy

Villers-Bocage

Bourguebus

Coutances

Thury Harcourt

Le Bény Bocage

Falaise

Villedieu

Granville

Vire

Condé sur Noireau

St Lambert

Chambois

Gacé

Laigle

Avranches

Flers

Argentan

Mortain

Barenton

Domfront

Sées

Dol

Fougeres

Mayenne

ALENCON

Mortagne

RENNES

Vitré

LAVAL

Mamers

Janzé

LE MANS

Vibraye

St Calais

187

ALLIED SUPPLIES FLOW IN

More troops and supplies were flowing over the beaches under the eyes of naval Beachmasters who never for a moment allowed the flow to slacken. 'Ducks' formed an endless belt, climbing up from the sea, going inland with their loads and passing back to the ships in the bay by another route.

The first of a number of old tankers and other ships had arrived, to be sunk close inshore to provide the beginnings of the 'Gooseberry' shelters which protected the hundreds of small craft and probably saved the expedition from disaster when the 'big gale' arose some days later. A start had been made, too, on the construction of the 'Mulberries', the prefabricated ports which had been planned to the last detail in England and towed to Normandy. Each concrete caisson displaced over six thousand tons, and something like a hundred and fifty of them had to be got into position. 'Mulberry A', intended for the Americans, was never completed, although it handled less than the expected load, the British 'Mulberry B' at Arromanches, at times handled as much as nine thousand tons of supplies in a day - three times as much as expected. But it was several weeks before 'Mulberry B' was working, and by then the Allied forces, with the ever present protection of the Air Forces, had accomplished wonders towards the build-up.

During the first three days of the operation alone, thirty-eight convoys, comprising seven hundred and forty-three ships and major landing craft, crossed the Channel with supplies and reinforcements which were landed on to the beaches into the charge of Beach Groups. This, of course, excludes the assault forces. Each Beach Group included stevedore companies who unloaded the cargo, Field Dressing Stations and Beach Dressing Stations of the Royal Army Medical Corps, Pioneer Companies, RAOC and RASC Beach Parties for running the stores dumps, Royal Corps of Signal sections, officers and men of the Army's Movement Control Branch; and each separate part of the Group had a small RAF detachment working alongside it to advise on the special RAF problems.

On June 19th 'the great gale' blew up and at once stopped all unloading to the beaches. The sea did not finally go down until June 23rd, but nonetheless, the position of the Expeditionary Force was never in doubt after the third day of the assault. By the tenth day half a million men and seventy-seven thousand vehicles had been landed. By the end of July over one million, six hundred thousand men, three hundred and forty thousand vehicles, and one million seven hundred thousand tons of stores had been landed.

The Beach Group had to organise the beaches and the immediate hinterland in order to land and then maintain the assault, follow up and build up formations. Beach organisation was the first step in the establishment and development of lines of communication and supply. The 'Beach Groups' responsibilities included the calling

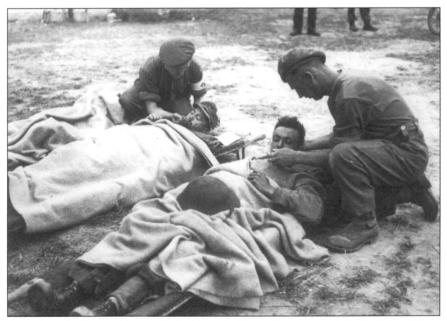

A wounded German is tended side by side with a wounded British soldier. Although this picture was obviously circulated for propaganda purposes, it is true to suggest that much less of the bitterness that characterised the war on the Russian Front was present during the Normandy Battles. Although some SS men were later tried for war crimes, the number of such incidents was remarkably small in relation to the scale of the fighting.

Based on the Volkswagen, the Kubelwagen was a small but very sturdy car, which was used extensively throughout the German Army.

in of the craft to beach in the correct order; the bringing ashore of all supplies and stores and all men and vehicles; the supervision of rearward movement and the embarkation of the wounded and prisoners of war for evacuation to Britain; the setting up and manning of anti aircraft guns and searchlights to protect the beaches and the ships off shore. The Beach Groups landed in Normandy with some of their engineers even before the first assault troops, and supplies continued to go in over the beaches until the Channel ports had been captured.

On most nights the Luftwaffe came and dropped bombs in the anchorage, but did little damage. During the day, on the few occasions when German planes appeared, they were always driven off by the ever present fighter patrols. In one conflict which might have been termed a battle, six FW190s were shot down for no Allied losses.

The Germans, in desperation, attempted to break into the anchorage with fairly powerful E-Boat forces operating from Cherbourg and Le Havre. This gave an opportunity to the 'little ships' of the Allies, and in the high speed actions which developed, they took a heavy toll of the German craft and eventually forced them to withdraw from Cherbourg. As many as seven of these naval actions in miniature were fought in a single night. Losses among Allied ships remained extremely light.

Less than a week after D-Day, on Monday, June 12th, the Prime Minister set foot on the beaches and made an extensive tour with General Montgomery: *"He made the final lap, as so many others had done, in a 'duck,' and was smoking a large cigar when he climbed down from the big boat-cum-vehicle. With him were Field Marshal Smuts and Field Marshal Sir Alan Brooke, Chief of the*

The German Nebelwerfer was a fearsome weapon - a multi-barrelled rocket-launcher which could bring down a ferocious bombardment at short notice. A disproportionately high number of Allied casualties in Normandy were caused by this weapon.

Imperial General Staff. All were given a great welcome by the troops; Mr Churchill's two fingers upraised in the Victory sign aroused the greatest enthusiasm."

The Luftwaffe made one of its few daylight attacks on the anchorage just before Mr. Churchill left to return to England, but their bombs fell harmlessly into the sea and then the raiders were chased inland by Spitfires.

The Americans, by this time, had a strong grip on the Germans to the west and British battle plans were taking shape in front of Caen. Still, every man, gun, and tank was needed, and the Navy and Merchant Navies continued to labour without ceasing to get them ashore.

'NO RETREAT!'

No battle ever follows a master plan to the last detail, but it was generally assumed by all the Allied commanders, including Montgomery, that once D-Day had succeeded and the Allies were safely ashore, they would make reasonably steady progress inland; and that the Germans would fall back in the face of their attack. That situation did not develop for a variety of reasons, but principally because, on 11th June, Adolf Hitler issued a 'No Retreat' order to his forces. The German high command must, by now, have had a sense of dread when they heard this instruction, which had resulted in the loss of huge German forces in North Africa and Russia.

The Allies were only a few miles inland from the original beaches when Hitler ordered his 'No Retreat' order. The Germans concentrated the bulk of their armour against the British forces and not the American forces. There were two principal reasons for this. One was that this was actually the best place for the Germans to group their armour for a possible attack down onto the beaches, had they ever been able to mount one. The other main reason was the British and Canadians, by persistently attacking on either side of Caen, posed the greatest threat of break-out from Normandy and the Germans always perceived this as the greatest danger.

This produced the situation in with the German armour concentrated against the British and Canadians. Much later, Montgomery and his staff were able to produce versions of plans which showed something which looked pretty much like that situation, with the British holding in the east, and the Americans breaking out in the west. But it is interesting to note that the plans had been based on holding territory much further inland than the actual circumstances dictated.

On the coast of Normandy, most of the shore batteries had

been either subdued or put out of action by the preliminary air bombardment on June 6th, and consequently opposition was less than expected. As we have seen, the seaborne landings on the east side of the Cotentin peninsula achieved almost complete surprise, but heavy seas and beach obstacles held up the initial landings on the beaches east of the Carentan estuary in the St Laurent district. Farther to the east and as far as the River Orne, the opposition to the initial assaults was patchy, but heavy inland fighting developed here as elsewhere, and enemy resistance stiffened as reserves came into action.

The Allied High Command had expected the German forces in Normandy to fight a slow retreat eastwards. Hitler's order to stand and fight regardless caught the Allies unprepared, and it took time before the great encirclement at Falaise was fully exercised.

HANDBOOK ON GERMAN MILITARY FORCES
EXTRACT NO.12
THE GERMAN ARMY IN RETREAT

"....Retreat is a forced retirement which is ordered by the Germans only when all possibilities for success are exhausted. The objective is to place enough distance between friendly and hostile forces to enable the former to conduct an orderly withdrawal and to occupy new positions to the rear.

COVERING FORCES

The Germans usually organise covering forces from troops in closest contact with the enemy, either whole tactical units or elements from several. These forces attempt to make the enemy believe that the position is still fully occupied. Engineers prepare additional obstacles, minefields, and booby traps forward of and within the positions to be held. A portion of the artillery and heavy infantry weapons support the covering forces. They maintain as long as possible their former fire activity to deceive the enemy, even when fulfilment of their mission means the loss of individual guns. The sector assigned to a covering force is usually too wide to be under effective control of a single commander, but the actions of the various commanders are closely co-ordinated. Orders specify whether the covering forces are to remain in contact with the hostile forces until they begin to advance, or to follow the main body after a specified interval.

As the distance from the enemy increases, the retiring troops form march columns.

REAR GUARD

Where possible, a division's retirement takes place along two parallel routes. The freshest troops available are used as rear guards. Since the rear guard cannot expect support from the retreating main body, it must be relatively strong. It is composed of infantry units. Generally the divisional field artillery retires with the main body, none being assigned to the rear guard. Self-propelled and heavy infantry-support guns, and even howitzers, are frequently attached to the rear guard. Tanks also may be assigned. A typical rear guard for each route in a division retirement is one infantry battalion, to which are attached elements of the reconnaissance unit, to protect the flanks, and of the engineer unit, to prepare demolitions.

German grenadiers go to ground in the face of Allied shell fire.

The rear guard infantry battalion normally employs only one of its rifle companies on active rear guard tasks. The three rifle companies perform this function in turn as long as their strength remains approximately even. If the terrain demands it, two companies are employed at a time. Two or more antitank guns and half of the self-propelled or heavy infantry guns allotted to the full rear guard support the rearmost rifle company or companies. When pressure becomes too strong, the single rifle company is withdrawn through the two remaining rifle companies, which are supported by the remainder of the attached weapons. Variations of this leapfrogging progress are repeated until darkness, when a general disengagement takes place and the original formation is resumed.

Rear guards withdraw by bounds to selected but not prepared positions. The extent to which positions eventually can be prepared depends on the proximity of the pursuing forces, the length of time each particular position is likely to be held, and the decision of the individual company and platoon commanders. During each stage of the retreat, the commander of the rear company can order a withdrawal to the main rear guard position, but withdrawal from each main rear guard position is ordered by the commander of the main body. Frequently the speed of withdrawal is based on a time-distance schedule. During the withdrawal from a certain town, rear guards were instructed to retire not more than three thousand yards a day.

Experience has shown that in certain types of country, a reinforced rear guard company generally can hold up very superior forces on a front as wide as three miles. In one instance of a withdrawal from a defensive position along a river line, a German Panzer division, which had one Panzer

Grenadier battalion and attached elements as its rear guard, was covered by one rifle company reinforced by a company of tanks, four infantry guns (including two self-propelled), and a battery of medium howitzers. The tanks were mainly used to cover the withdrawal of the rifle elements. On another occasion a similar rear party had a number of heavy mortars attached. These covered the infantry withdrawal with the help of four tanks, which also carried the mortars back to the next bound.

Particularly suited for rear guard tasks, because of its armour and high fire power, is the armoured reconnaissance battalion of the Panzer division. When employing the armoured reconnaissance battalion in terrain that affords cover, the Germans site well camouflaged, armoured halftracks in wooded areas, flat reverse slopes, or high grain fields, and open fire with all weapons at very close range. The armoured half-tracks then penetrate into the confused enemy and, after repulsing him, retreat to previously organised alternate positions....."

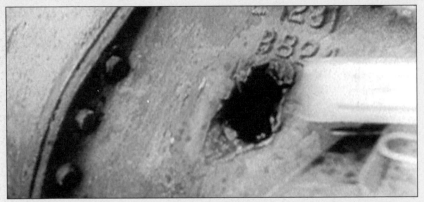

A close up frame from a German newsreel demonstrates just how effective the Panzerfaust could be at short ranges. This hole was punched in the frontal armour of a Sherman tank. The shot which entered the tank was fired at a range of fifty yards or less.

"By the evening of the 6th, advance elements of the assault divisions were some few miles inland of the beaches to the east and west of Port en Bessin, the following towns and villages having been captured: St Martin, St Laurent, Colleville, Arromanches, Ryes, Creully, Tailleville and Ranville. Ste Mere Eglise was captured by US airborne troops. A bridgehead approximately twenty-five miles wide was established, which was quickly joined with the lodgement to the west to form one continuous front, with American forces in the Cotentin peninsula and just east of the Vire, Canadian and British troops on the left flank."

The bridgehead was steadily extended, and after Bayeux had been captured in the British sector on the 7th, an armoured thrust in the direction of Villers-Bocage secured a deep salient extending just south of Tilly sur Seulles, (eight miles southeast of Bayeux). To the east, British troops advanced to within three miles of Caen, while to the west US forces penetrated to a depth of five miles south

A German officer inspects the damage to Allied vehicles which occurred during the battle of Villers-Bocage.

The crew of British heavy gun labour into the night to supply fire support for the advancing infantry. The Allied superiority in artillery was to play a major part in the Normandy campaign.

of Colleville and crossed the River Aure to the east of Trevieres. Isigny, (six miles east of Carentan) was captured on the 9th, together with the high ground to the west, thus completing the contact with the lodgement in the Cotentin peninsula. On the morning of the 12th, Carentan fell to U S troops who entered Montebourg on the following day, but were forced to give ground before the town, devastated in the fighting, was finally captured on the 19th of June.

Violent fighting, in which strong armoured forces were engaged by both sides, continued on all fronts, and many important positions changed hands several times.

"It was the first time that the 5th Battalion of the Duke of Cornwall's Light Infantry had had a taste of battle and again the tanks had gone amongst them, so everyone was scattered all over the place and with difficulty I managed to find the company's headquarters. They were in a farmyard. I eventually found it, but

just before I found it I came across a sergeant in a ditch crying his eyes out because he had lost all his men, and he sat there weeping. I thought, how extraordinary, these sergeants, we see them on the drill, and they are all brave and stout men, but when it comes to the battlefield he was weeping like a child. However, I expect he recovered himself and got used to it. It was just that first, initial shock, I think, that upset him. Evidently he did care for the men that he had got under his command.

Anyway, when I got to company headquarters, the Company Commander said that there were some fellows that had been killed over in a copse about one hundred yards down the road and he said 'Would you go and prepare them for burial.' So I went down to this copse with another fellow and took these fellow's personal belongings off them and made the tabs out for them. We put them into sacks for burial and I found one of them was my pal. We'd been pals since we'd left the Royal Warwickshire Regiment, so I had the job of preparing him for burial. That was the my initiation to the Battle of Normandy.

German prisoners in a prisoner of war camp queue for food. This image gives an impression of the huge number of German prisoners captured at the beginning of the Normandy battles.

A Sherman tank which was hit and caught fire in the battle of Villers-Bocage.

The company commander had been killed; he went up into a tree to recce the ground and a sniper shot him, so there was a bit of confusion during that battle. I was there with the twelve others for three days and we should have only been there just over the one day. How I escaped getting hit there, I really don't know, because out of the six hundred men that went in from the Duke of Cornwall's, when we came to muster up after the three days, we only counted twenty-five of us. So you can tell the heat of the battle. Nearly a hundred were buried on the spot on the hill. The opposition was German Tigers that we had then. All the German tanks, even the Panthers were very quiet, they were very stealthy. I think they must have been named Tigers and Panthers because they were very stealthy, they crept up on you, next minute there was one coming round the corner and you didn't hear it, whereas our own Churchills and Shermans kicked such a hell of a row you could hear them a mile away. And the Churchills were even worse, because they used to throw up dust when it was dry, and when it was wet they churned it up and made the going very heavy for us infantry. We were glad, however, of the Shermans because they cleared the minefields with the flails, so we were rather grateful when they came. They were also used as flamethrowers to get the snipers, because there were snipers in foxholes and the only way to get them out was the flamethrower. It must have been a horrible death, but I should think it must have been pretty well instantaneous."

In the Caen area especially, German resistance stiffened, but no co-ordinated German counter-attack developed. This was partly due to the fact that the infantry component of the Panzer divisions had had to be committed immediately on arrival in the battle area, while Allied air action against communications and activity by the French Forces of the Interior had considerably slowed down the rate of enemy reinforcement. In fact, the German rate of build-up fell short of original estimates, and in particular they lacked sufficient infantry to hold ground.

As a result of a powerful thrust, British tanks and infantry captured Villers-Bocage on the 13th of June, but that small success was to provoke a vicious response.

RETROGRADE MOVEMENTS

WITHDRAWAL FROM ACTION

"...The Germans break off an engagement for one or more of the following reasons: when it has served its purpose; when conditions require the employment of the troops, or part of them, on another front; when a continuation of the battle gives no promise of success; or when defeat is imminent.

When an attack exhausts itself without attaining its objective, the Germans assume the defensive as the first step in withdrawing from action. If the defence must be continued in a rearward position, the breaking of contact, the retirement, and the resumption of the defence are carefully planned beforehand. Positions in the rear are prepared for the reception of the troops, particularly if they have been engaged in heavy fighting. The retirement is made in conjunction with that of adjacent units, and stress

German grenadiers move forward to the attack under cover of a smoke screen. Smoke was used to cover retreats and withdrawals.

is placed on maintaining the cohesiveness of the retiring forces.

By maintaining the usual fire of all arms, the Germans try to deceive their enemy as long as possible as to the continued occupation in force of their original position.

In view of the severe losses inflicted by Allied planes and armoured forces on German troops during daylight disengagements, the Germans try to await darkness before withdrawing from action. At night they break off combat on a wide front and move back along routes as nearly perpendicular as possible to terrain features suitable for fighting delaying actions. When the situation forces them to withdraw during daylight, they do so by unit sectors, coordinating the movements of adjacent units.

ORDERS

The German company commander follows this outline in drafting his orders for breaking off an engagement:

General instructions:

- Rearward movement of supplies, ammunition-carrying vehicles, and equipment.
- Reconnaissance and marking of routes of withdrawal.

Detailed instructions:

- Combat orders for the covering forces (reconnaissance units, heavy support weapons, medical personnel, infantry combat wagons, and infantry engineers).
- Type, time, and march order for the withdrawal of the rifle platoons and heavy weapons.
- Assembly areas.
- Location of the company commander....."

A German prisoner wearing a camouflaged smock is taken into captivity by a US infantry man. The smock was generally issued to snipers, and in this case, the young man is probably lucky to have escaped with his life.

- CHAPTER 11 -
OPERATION 'PERCH'

The countryside around Villers-Bocage is typical of the terrain which soon gained the infamous nickname the 'Green Hell'. Most of the Normandy countryside was, and still is, a beautiful natural chequerboard of fields marked with higher banks topped with hedges. Dotted throughout the landscape were medieval villages, with churches which inevitably featured tall towers, and strong farms which had specifically been built for defence in medieval times. This formed a unique combination of man-made and natural defence systems, with communication ditches running along the main length of the fields. The hedgerow country or, in French, the Bocage, was a formidable aid to the Germans in their defence.

In the Bocage, it was easy to lose one's bearings and since the Allies depended very heavily on artillery and on airpower, not just to break through but to hold their own casualties down, it was extremely hard for them to direct that firepower with complete accuracy. One Royal Artillery observer is supposed to have solved this problem by simply calling down fire on what he thought was his own position and spotting where the shells actually landed, about a mile away. If true, this was probably a rather drastic but effective way of locating one's position.

The fighting in the Bocage was, in the most simple terms, extremely time consuming and manpower intensive. In a network of closely packed small fields, with dense hedges and high banks and narrow lanes running between them, the Germans found themselves possessing an absolutely perfect defensive position. The stoutly built Norman farmhouses and villages which were sprinkled across Normandy, usually had cellars which provided good cover for the Germans. Inevitably, it was going to take considerable time and indeed considerable losses to push the Germans out of this massively strong defensive position.

Essentially, the only way to push through a defended Bocage position, was to bring down massive fire power from the air and from artillery onto the German positions. The forward positions would be lightly held and the Allied forces therefore had often to guess where the more strongly defended rear positions were, and then break through along the line of the hedgerows. This task was made somewhat easier in the middle of the battle when the Americans came up with a special attachment to fit to the front of the tank, the Rhinoceros attachment, enabling them to drive through the hedgerows rather than over. But essentially it was a slow grinding battle, very much like the jungle warfare of the Pacific or even the trench warfare of the first World War and casualty rates were comparable. The British were losing infantry at about the same

A dead German grenadier lies among the debris of the streets of a shattered French town. Although Allied losses were high, by this stage of the war, German losses were becoming irreplaceable.

HANDBOOK ON GERMAN MILITARY FORCES
EXTRACT NO.14
MOBILE STEEL PILLBOXES

"....The Germans also have a mobile steel pillbox (see figures 1 and 2 below) which is armed with a machine gun and manned by two men. The pillbox is constructed in two sections, a top half and a bottom half welded together. The top half contains the aperture, armament, air vents, and entrance door. Thickness of the armour varies from five inches at the aperture to two inches at the sides and top. The bottom half is only three-quarters of an inch thick, but is entirely below ground level when the pillbox is in place.

The total weight of the pillbox without armament or ammunition is 6,955 pounds. The aperture, which is seen on the left side in the photograph, is divided into two parts:

Figures 1 and 2.

the lower part for the gun barrel; the upper for sighting. The machine gun has an arc of fire of approximately forty-five degrees. The aperture cover is operated manually from the interior of the pillbox. Entry is through a door, twenty by twenty-three inches, in the back of the upper half. The door can be seen hanging open on the right in the photograph. There are two openings in the top for periscopes, one over each seat.

A blower operated by a pedal provides ventilation. The ventilation holes on both sides of the pillbox also enable an axle to be passed through the pillbox. Wheels are fitted to the ends of this axle and the pillbox can then be towed upside down. When installed for use, the sides and top are banked to blend with the surroundings...."

A German grenadier blends in with the foliage in the Bocage country. He is carrying two hand held anti-tank weapons, which were deadly and effective at short ranges and were ideally suited to the nature of the Bocage countryside.

The aftermath of RAF attack on German transport equipment at Rouen, August 1944.

rate in Normandy as they had on the Somme or at Passchendaele in the First World War. What was noticeable was that although the Allies made only small advances even in a big attack, they might make two or three thousand yards, into a German position. Then the whole thing would quickly come to a halt after German counter-attacks. Once they lost that ground, however, the Germans had the same problem. They were never able to mount a counter attack of their own which pushed the Allies back to any serious extent. So whoever held the Bocage ground was is in a very strong position. As the battle developed, however, once the Germans lost ground, they could not hope to recover it.

"Well the problem in the north of the Bocage for anybody who had visited it, is that the hedges are on top of sort of, what you might call, earth walls. So when a tank tries to climb over these walls, it exposes its underbelly and the German tanks which have very superior armaments and were able to dig in behind these walls

further back, and pick them off. So I think this was a very, very difficult area in which to conduct armoured warfare; much easier to conduct defensive infantry warfare. Attacking was a nightmare."

As we have seen, Montgomery had taken the decision to bypass Caen if possible and aim for the town of Villers-Bocage. It was here that the Tiger tanks of 101 SS Battalion would make their reputation. Among them was Michael Wittman, one of the most famous tank commanders of all time, and the greatest Panzer leader in the German army. His crew had been credited with an incredible number of kills in Russia, something like one hundred and twenty enemy fighting vehicles had already been credited to their Tiger. The British forces now planned to make a wide sweeping movement around the back of the Panzer Lehr Division which had been given the name of Operation 'Perch', but the British were not aware that fourteen Tiger tanks were now in the vicinity of Villers-Bocage.

A British Churchill tank rumbles through the ruins of a French village. The destroyed vehicle is a German Mark IV tank. The object in the foreground is the turret of the tank which has been blown off by the force of the explosion.

212

HANDBOOK ON GERMAN MILITARY FORCES
EXTRACT NO.15
ANTI-TANK DEFENCES

"....In constructing a defensive position the Germans stress construction of obstacles and antitank defenses. If possible they select tank-proof terrain, and natural tank obstacles, such as steep slopes, are improved. Originally the Germans constructed antitank ditches well forward of the main line of resistance, but experience taught them that such ditches offered favourable jumping-off positions for hostile infantry and also revealed the location of the main line of resistance. At the present time, therefore, antitank ditches normally, are dug in the area between the main line of resistance and the artillery positions. They are built in an uninterrupted line to avoid leaving passages that can be exploited by the enemy. All crossings essential to assure the manoeuvrability of friendly troops are built so that they can be blown up on the shortest notice.

One of the original illustrations from the handbook illustrates an 88mm anti-aircraft gun pressed into the anti-tank role. The boxes in the foreground are for the bulky 88mm ammunition.

The sighting device used for aiming the 88mm gun. The German forces enjoyed an advantage over the Allies in the manufacture of optical devices, for which German industry was renowned.

The Germans are aware that obstacles of any kind are effective only when covered by fire from various weapons. Consequently, there usually are trenches behind the antitank ditches from which machine-gun and antitank-gun fire can cover the entire length of the tank obstacle.

The Germans learned that dense minefields in front of their positions were an inadequate tank obstacle, because the enemy usually neutralised them by massed artillery fire or by concentrated air bombardment before launching a large-scale attack. Now German minefields normally are laid within the main battle position, and only single mines are dispersed in patterns at wide intervals in front of the main line of resistance. Particular stress is placed on the mining of roads. Routes of withdrawal which have to be left open are prepared for mining, and, if time does not permit placing of actual mines, dummy mines are installed.

The Germans employ many kinds of tank obstacles. They recently have used static flame throwers dug into the ground. Usually sited in pairs and in conjunction with other tank obstacles, they are fired by well concealed personnel as soon as hostile tanks come within range.

German antitank guns are disposed in depth, with some well forward. They often are dug in and carefully concealed to prevent the enemy from discovering the location and strength of the antitank defenses prior to attack. In emplacing antitank guns, the Germans prefer positions in enfilade or on reverse slopes. They normally employ two to three antitank guns in each position, protecting them from infantry attacks with light machine guns. Ranges at which the Germans open fire upon hostile tanks vary according to the calibre of the gun and its position. Although single antitank guns sometimes engage enemy tanks at ranges up to one thousand yards, main antitank defenses usually hold their fire until the range is reduced to about a hundred and

Another view of the 88mm dual purpose gun, from the Handbook on German Military Forces.

fifty to three hundred yards. The employment of close-combat antitank teams, supplements the antitank defence. When the hostile tank attack is repulsed, the antitank guns move to alternate positions.

The Germans emphasise that the use of smoke can be of great assistance in defeating enemy tank attacks. Smoke shells are fired into the attacking formation about one-third the distance back from the leading echelon. Thus the Germans avoid blinding their own antitank gunners, and leading hostile tanks not only are left without adequate support but are silhouetted against the smoke. The Germans also rely on the smoke being sucked into the tanks and forcing the crews to dismount."

Dead German grenadiers litter the streets of Cherbourg in the aftermath of the fierce fighting for the port.

In an attempt to outflank these stubborn defenders at Carpiquet, Montgomery dispatched his highly experienced 7th Armoured Division, the Desert Rats, to make a broad sweep south of Caen which was scheduled to begin on June 12th.

The battle of Villers-Bocage, which took place over 13th and 14th June, involved significant elements of the 7th armoured division who were opposed by numerically inferior German forces. Incredible as it now seems, on 13th June Michael Wittman with a few German machines brought the British 7th Armoured Division to a complete halt. The British armoured column had stopped to make tea when Michael Wittman's single Tiger emerged from cover and after knocking out a rear tank, drove down the column at a range as close as fifty yards, destroying the vehicles as they went. Wittman then continued on into Villers-Bocage where he knocked out three Stuart tanks. In the centre of the town his tank was immobilised by a British anti-tank gun. Nonetheless, Wittman and his crew managed to escape across the fields and make their way seven kilometres to the headquarters of Panzer Lehr at Aurbois to the north of Villers-Bocage. There he reported to the Divisional Commander then and turned about with fifteen Panzer IV's and once more headed into the attack.

Wittman used the Panzer IV's to set up a blocking position to the north of Villers-Bocage. The British losses that day included twenty Cromwells, four Firefly Shermans, three Stuarts, sixteen personnel carriers, fourteen half tracks and two six pounder anti-tank guns.

The defeat of the 7th Armoured Division at Villers-Bocage represented the loss of the last real opportunity to make the battle for Normandy the mobile battle which the Allied planners hoped, and indeed expected, that it would be. In this respect it has to be said that the battle appears to have been badly mismanaged by the British Corps Commander, Lieutenant General Bucknell, who failed, by his sluggishness and lack of a proactive flexible approach, to reinforce the lead armoured brigade of 7th Armoured Division at a moment in the battle where it could still, despite its early setback, have achieved

British troops cautiously pick their way through the rubble of a devastated French town.

a decisive outflanking of the German position in Normandy. This is clearly a case where British command and control, and in particular the command and control by one man, was deficient. The British withdrew to the high ground east of Caumont, where the Americans, who were in touch with the British forces, had expanded their difficult St Laurent bridgehead to a depth of some twenty miles.

THE AMERICAN FRONT

The primary American objective, however, was to seal off the Cotentin peninsula, at the same time strengthening the southern flank of the salient to prevent the enemy relieving his formations cut off in the north. The Americans made slow progress until the 15th, when leading US troops entered St Sauveur Le Vicomte (captured next day). Thereafter opposition slackened and they reached the west coast of the peninsula on the 18th at Barreville-sur-Mer.

A German grenadier armed with the effective MG42 machine gun which was introduced into service in 1942. Its high rate of fire meant the MG42 was much feared by the Allies.

HANDBOOK ON GERMAN MILITARY FORCES
EXTRACT NO.16
DELAYING ACTION

"....The Germans make a distinction between "delaying engagements" (Hinhaltendes Gefecht) and "delaying action" (Hinhaltender Widerstand). A delaying engagement is primarily the general plan of the higher commander for holding back the enemy. Delaying actions are the measures taken by lower units to carry out the higher commander's plan.

The purpose of delaying actions is to enable the main German force to disengage itself from battle, retire in order, and establish a new defensive position. Delaying actions therefore seek to deceive the enemy as to German strength, dispositions, and intentions; to prevent the enemy from committing the main German forces; and to prevent close pursuit of the main forces by the enemy. These measures are accomplished by rear guards, special battle groups, and strongpoints, all of which are characterised by high automatic fire power, mobility, and economy in numerical strength.

Delaying actions are organised not in a main defensive belt, but on lines of resistance (Widerstandslinien). The distance between such lines is great enough to prevent the enemy from engaging two of them from the same artillery position. He is compelled to displace and move up his artillery to engage each line. These lines of resistance are normally established along forward slopes to facilitate disengagement and withdrawal under cover. The delaying actions are fought forward of the lines of resistance with patrols-every effort is made to destroy such patrols-but only when the enemy mounts an attack. If it can be ascertained that the enemy is preparing for a massed attack, the Germans make a timely withdrawal to avoid exposing the troops to enemy artillery concentrations. Advance elements employ smoke to enable them to make a getaway in a critical situation. Riflemen cover the disengagement of heavy weapons, which move back by bounds. Every opportunity is taken to make limited counterattacks in order to inflict casualties on an enemy who advances recklessly.

Fire is opened at extreme ranges on an enemy advancing for a major attack. Enemy reconnaissance forces are allowed to approach, however, and then an effort is made to destroy them.

Counter-attacks on a large scale are avoided, except when the enemy threatens to penetrate the line of resistance. When that occurs, the Germans counter-attack with the main forces of the rear guard and seek to restore the situation in order that the program of staged withdrawal

German engineers involved in the construction of concrete defences.

mobile forces. Furthermore, battle Outposts are organised forward of each line.

The main delaying weapons are machine guns, mortars, and self-propelled weapons. Tanks are used in small groups.

Maintenance of contact is a most conspicuous principle in the Germans' conduct of a withdrawal and delaying action. The size, composition, direction, and intention of the attacking enemy force are observed at all times.

CONDUCT OF THE DELAYING ACTION

During a delaying action, wide sectors are covered by artillery units widely deployed-guns are sited by sections if necessary-and by widely distributed infantry-support weapons. The defence is then further organised by establishing strongpoints manned by small groups.

The positions from which delaying actions are fought are characterised by very slight depth. As a general rule, a unit is responsible for double the front normally allocated in defensive fighting. A company sector is six hundred and fifty to thirteen hundred yards; a battalion sector one thousand seven hundred and fifty to four thousand four hundred yards; a regimental sector four thousand four hundred to six thousand six hundred yards; and a division sector thirteen thousand to twenty-two thousand yards.

In leaving a line of resistance, German covering forces attempt to disengage by night. If that is not possible, their actions are governed by the following principle: the enemy is not allowed to come closer to them than they are from their next line of resistance. The troops must be able to reach the new position before the enemy reaches the old one, or their losses will be excessive.

The troops therefore do not retire in the face of enemy

may be continued. Local counter-attacks are made for the protection or retention of some feature essential to the safe conduct of the main withdrawal, or to gain time for the preparation of the line of resistance or phase line.

The area between the lines of resistance is called the intermediate area (Zwischenfeld). Explicit orders are given as to whether the intermediate area is to be covered in one bound or is to be fought over. The latter necessity arises especially when the next line of resistance has not been fully prepared and time must be gained. Detachments must reach the line of resistance early enough to insure that all the main positions are occupied in time.

The supply of ammunition is carefully organised. A great deal of ammunition is required for delaying actions because a few weapons on a broad front must do as much as or even more than the normal number of guns in a defensive position. When ammunition is scarce, the Germans specify, down to sections if necessary, the quantity of ammunition that may be used at each position. Every commander maintains a supply of ammunition for emergencies.

The Germans stress the importance of deceiving the enemy by every means. Artillery and heavy weapons are moved continually to give an impression of greater strength. Dummy positions and camouflage are also widely used.

So that isolated groups may be adequately directed, signal communication receives special attention.

In delaying actions in mountainous terrain, the Germans make greater use of their reconnaissance and engineer units than of any other component. Reconnaissance units are almost continuously in contact with advance and flanking enemy elements, and participate in most rear-guard and battle-group engagements....."

General Carl Wilhelm von Schlieben, Commander of the German Forces in Cherbourg, and Rear-Admiral Hennecke, Sea Defence Commandant for Normandy, arrive at General Collins's H.Q. to surrender. The last strongpoint in Cherbourg fell on June 27, 1944.

One of the overriding requirements for Allied success in Normandy was the capture of a port to allow the build up to proceed much faster. Cherbourg was the obvious target. The port was held for the Germans by a sixteen thousand strong garrison under General Carl Wilhem von Schlieben. It was to be attacked by Lieutenant General Omar Bradley's US 1st army. Although the action at Utah Beach had been relatively easy on D-Day, once again the difficult Bocage country made the American drive towards Cherbourg a dangerous and undeniably costly plod. The American response was to strike across country to seal off the Cotentin peninsula with a drive to the town of Barnaville, which they reached on June 18th.

THE BATTLE FOR CHERBOURG

With Montebourg and Bricquebec firmly secured by the 19th, the Americans found themselves within ten miles of Cherbourg, and faced by elements of three German infantry divisions. They reached the main defences on the 21st, encountering fierce resistance from prepared positions. Intensive aerial bombardment and artillery fire on the 25th assisted the US 7th Corps to extend its initial penetration of the outskirts of the town; while on the same day other American troops reached the coast at St Vaast and Barfleur and made further advances on the opposite flank. By the 26th, fierce street fighting was in progress in Cherbourg, during which General Carl Wilhelm von Schlieben, Commander of the German forces in Cherbourg, and Rear Admiral Hennecke, Sea Defence Commandant for Normandy, were captured. On the 27th, the last strongpoint in the naval arsenal surrendered and resistance in the town ended.

The German garrison of Cherbourg finally surrendered and the last elements gave up the fight on June 29th. Some die-hards fighting in the Cap de la Hague soldiered on, but by then the whole of the rest of the Cotentin Peninsula had been cleared.

Adolf Hitler had given personal instructions to Schlieben that

"Even if the worst comes to the worst it is your duty to defend Cherbourg to the last bunker and to leave the enemy not a harbour but a field of ruins." Schlieben had done his duty and the Allies were stunned to find just how thoroughly and comprehensively the harbour at Cherbourg had been destroyed.

With typical teutonic thoroughness the Germans had laid mines, sunk block ships and methodically destroyed all of the harbour facilities. The approaches to the port of Cherbourg and the harbour itself had been heavily mined, and the quays and docks were found extensively damaged, but certain hards and beaches were quickly turned to use for landing of troops and supplies, pending the restoration of the more important harbour facilities. Cherbourg was effectively closed as a port until September, and by then the fight had moved on. The battle for the Cotentin peninsula had cost the Americans eighteen hundred dead and fifteen thousand wounded. In return they had captured forty thousand German prisoners and were now poised to begin to strike southwards.

German troops defending the Maupertus aerodrome, seven miles east of the town, and small pockets in the Cap de la Hague still held

Allied fighters operated from forward airstrips in France.

out, and it was not until July 1st that the north of the peninsula was firmly in Allied hands.

As soon as the Allied armies had gained a foothold in Normandy, work had begun on the construction of the Mulberry harbours. The block ships were sunk and in use by June 11th. By June 18th more than half the caissons were in position. But as we have seen, on June 19th 'the gale' blew up from the north-east and continued for three days. Mulberry A, intended for the Americans, was badly damaged, and was never completed, although the capture of Cherbourg reduced its importance. The British Mulberry B at Arromanches, protected to some extent by the Calvados reef, suffered less damage, though the gale took a heavy toll. Nonetheless, during this critical period, when the storms made unloading on to open beaches impossible, a small but important trickle of stores was landed in the Arromanches harbour. Even on the worst day, eight hundred tons of petrol and ammunition as well as many troops, got ashore over the piers. A long spell of rough weather followed the gale, and the harbour was not unloading to maximum capacity until July. Scheduled to handle seven thousand tons a day, it thereafter at times handled as much as nine thousand tons daily. It remained in operation until November, when the great port of Antwerp came into use.

FIERCE FIGHTING

In the British sector intensive fighting continued, but the general line remained unaltered. On June 16th, HMS Ramillies bombarded German armour north-cast of Caen, while three US battleships gave fire support to American troops near Isigny and Carentan. More German armour was shelled on the 18th by HMS Diadem, on which date SHAEF announced that the enemy battery at Houlgate, (east of Ouistreham), had been silent for thirty-six hours after bombardment by HMS Ramillies. Shelling of enemy targets by Allied warships continued.

OPERATION 'EPSOM'

After the failure of Operation 'Perch', there was a lull in the fighting on the British sector between the 18th and 24th of June, when the German divisional accounts describe the front as being relatively quiet. Nonetheless, a steady flow of casualties began to drain the lifeblood away from the German divisions and there were simply no longer any reinforcements to bring relief. There were, in fact, some attempts to bring in relief forces but that had to be done at the expense of weakening the Eastern Front.

Paul Hausser's 2nd SS Panzer Corps, which included the 9th and 10th SS Panzer Divisions, was ordered from Poland to France on 10th June, but an undertaking of such magnitude took a considerable time and they could not be expected in the battle area before 25th June at the earliest. Also summoned to fight in Normandy were the SS Leibstandarte which had to come from Belgium. This, too, proved an extremely difficult and hazardous journey, both from the lack of fuel and the incessant Allied air attacks. One new division of reinforcements which did arrive was the 2nd SS Panzer Division, Das Reich. They reached the battle area after a notorious march from the south, which had seen vicious reprisals against French civilians in response to attacks on the marching columns by the French resistance.

Montgomery now decided that, after the failure of the battle around Villers-Bocage, he would launch a hammer blow against the western defences of Caen. This operation was given the code name, 'Epsom'. It was originally scheduled to begin on 23rd June, but the famous storm which disrupted the flow of supplies meant that the operation had to be postponed until 25th June. This respite gave the Germans a much needed time to bring up their reinforcements and on 24th June, elements of the 1st SS Panzer Division, Leibstandarte,

OPERATION EPSOM

Operation Epsom was designed to use the superior weight of the British armoured forces to punch a hole in the German defences to the west of Caen. This was designed to lead to a series of enveloping attacks resulting in the fall of the city.

Epsom was thwarted by a series of German armoured counter-attacks which were rigorously pursued by elements of the first SS Panzer Corps who managed to limit the British penetration to depths of some five miles. A number of gains were surrendered when the British 11th Armoured Division were forced to withdraw on the 30th of June.

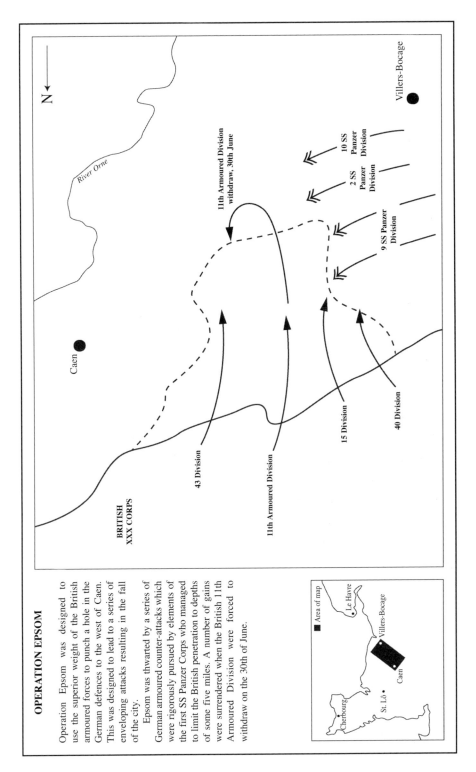

began to be unloaded from their train from Belgium. Allied air attacks were making travel almost impossible and although some elements began to arrive in time to take part in the 'Epsom' battles, it was to be the 6th July before the whole division could be concentrated on the area of the battlefield.

The operational plan for Operation 'Epsom' certainly had its limitations. The plan called for the main attack to be carried out by three divisions of the 8th Corps. Two of these divisions were infantry, and one was armoured. They would be committed on a very narrow front between Carpiquet airfield and Rourie to the west. This meant that the three divisions would be compacted into very small areas, much of which was typical of the very difficult Bocage country. Almost unbelievably, all the important roads, railways and rivers in the line of attack ran directly across the line of advance, which gave the defenders a huge advantage. Nonetheless, the British must have felt confident, as General Sir Richard O'Connor's 8th Corps was a very powerful formation. In addition to having its full

A poignant reminder of the ever-present danger of sudden death for the soldiers on both sides.

The special AVRE version of the Churchill tank rumbles through a village in Normandy. After the capture of the initial objectives on D-Day, AVRE continued to demonstrate its effectiveness in combat against fixed defences.

compliment of sixty thousand men and six hundred tanks, it was also supported by a huge assemblage of artillery which amounted to over nine hundred field pieces. In addition, the Royal Navy's support could be counted on and fighter bombers of 2nd Tactical Airforce were also on hand. This, of course, was the same General Richard O'Connor who had been captured in the desert and had now been freed from captivity by Italy's departure from the war. O'Connor had taken advantage of the chaos surrounding Italys exit from the war and escaped from his Italian POW camp. He was now given senior command again.

The main German defenders who were to receive the weight of Operation Epsom were elements of the 12th SS Panzer Division Hitler Jugend. Despite the losses that Hitler Jugend had already endured, they still had a considerable force which was able to be fielded. On 16th June, their strength was fifty-eight Mark IV tanks and forty-four Panthers. In addition another thirty tanks were undergoing repair and were expected to be operational again within the very near future. Early on the morning of June 26th a massive Allied artillery barrage commenced the battle, and wave after wave of fighter bombers took to the sky to support the operation. The intention was for the artillery to produce a First World War style creeping wall of fire, behind which the infantry could advance in the same manner as they had done at the Somme.

Operation 'Epsom' was a major British attack to the west of Caen, with its initial objective a hill called Hill 112. If the British could have secured command of this, they would have commanded the area to the west. Drawing up plans for any battle, there is always the greatest possibility of success if everything works; if everything had gone absolutely perfectly, the British would have carried on to the south of Caen. After three days of very hard fighting they were stopped short, holding the northern slopes of Hill 112. The British had therefore achieved about half their objectives.

In this frame from a German newsreel, two grenadiers are caught in the process of stalking Allied Sherman tanks. The Panzerfaust used by the man on the right was highly effective over the short ranges at which many of these battles were fought.

German casualties litter the dense hedgerows of the Bocage country.

Gordon Mucklow vividly recalled the fighting.

"Then the next battle was at Hill 112 near Escay Thorodon, it was later re-named Cornwall Hill, because so many Cornishmen were lost. By then, I had joined the 5th Battalion the Duke of Cornwall's Light Infantry. They were mostly Cornishmen, so of course I was a stranger, being a Warwickshire man amongst the Cornishmen. That was the battle that Rommel said, 'whoever captures Hill 112 will win the battle for France.'

We were opposed by SS Panzers and we had quite a battle with them. We went onto the hill and I was right in the forward edge of an orchard and when I got there, one of the fellas had got a German machine gun and he was using rounds of ammunition so fast I said 'we shall have no ammunition left if you carry on like that.' He said, 'go and grab a Bren gun.' There were twelve of us and we all each had a Bren gun we took from the dead bodies off the field and we stuffed our blouses with magazines. We held two German attacks off that night and the following day and we were shelled and mortared during the night and we survived."

One of the reasons the Allied advance halted, was that signals intelligence had discovered that an important German reserve formation, the 2nd SS Panzer Corps of two divisions, which had just detrained from the eastern front, was going to be committed into the flank of the 'Epsom' drive in an attempt to destroy it. The attack was halted in order to absorb the counter-attack.

"We were the last of the reserves and therefore there was no-one to relieve us. We were able to equip ourselves with Bren guns and each one of us, twenty of us, had all got Bren guns each, so we held the Germans off for those three days. We must have killed quite a few Germans on that Hill as well. In fact their casualties were greater than ours, so it must have been terrific."

It took the employment of five German armoured divisions to stop 'Epsom', four of them from the SS. In the process, the German Commander of 7th Army, General Dolman, who was absolutely convinced that it was going to break through, committed suicide in desperation.

German SS Officers study their maps and plan the next move. This study depicts an uncharacteristically relaxed group in a campaign which grew increasingly difficult for the German commanders.

A vivid example of the destructive power of Allied air and naval bombardment; only the heavy concrete casemate of this German shore battery remains intact.

Operation 'Epsom' was at the very least a semi-successful British attack in Normandy; it certainly helped to pin German Panzer formations in position and, as is frequently the case, to describe it as a failure is perhaps a trifle unfair. Nevertheless it is clear that Operation 'Epsom' demonstrated a number of failings on the part of the British forces participating, in particular in terms of deficiencies in liaison and co-ordination between the two British corps involved, 30 Corps and 8 Corps.

"We went into Hill 112, about six hundred men, and we had fire, machine gun bullets from each side of the Hill and we went through that. How I escaped that, I don't know. We had a Canadian officer with us and he said, 'look fellas, the German grenades have got long fuses on them. So when they land near you, pick them up and throw them back.' So of course we did. We actually went up to a machine gun nest and they threw these grenades at us, we threw them back and they ran like mad. They realised what was happening and the

HANDBOOK ON GERMAN MILITARY FORCES
EXTRACT NO.17
COMBAT IN WOODS

"....When attacking in woods, the Germans usually divide the area into company sectors. The Germans stress constant reconnaissance to discover the most weakly manned enemy position. This reconnaissance is carried out, even though company strength becomes temporarily reduced. Reconnaissance patrols usually move clockwise from their original position. The company commander reviews the reconnaissance reports in detail with his platoon and section leaders.

Heavily disguised with branches in an attempt to conceal it from the air, a German tank rumbles through the hedgerows towards the frontline.

The company usually deploys in wedge formation when advancing. In order to achieve surprise, the Germans often leave the roads and advance cross-country.

As soon as the point of the wedge of the company is in sight of the enemy, the Germans creep forward to close-combat range, always keeping contact with adjacent and supporting units. The company then storms the enemy's position, using the greatest possible number of hand grenades, pole charges, and close-combat weapons. The advance elements attempt to break into the hostile position as deeply as possible, the body of the wedge widening the penetration on both sides. The company commander then decides whether to roll up the enemy position on the more important flank or to hold the ground until reinforcements arrive before continuing the attack.

Each platoon details at least one observer, armed with an automatic weapon, to neutralise enemy tree top snipers. The Germans believe that bursts of fire, rather than single shots, are necessary to deal effectively with such snipers.

The Germans consider fighting in wooded areas as the primary task of riflemen and machine gunners, since the employment of heavy-support weapons often is impossible. The Germans occasionally dismount heavy machine guns and use them as light machine guns. Antitank guns of small calibre and light infantry howitzers sometimes are brought forward manually, and when indirect fire is not possible they engage targets directly. Light mortars are employed individually. From Finnish troops, the Germans learned a successful method of using mortars in woods. The mortar observers, accompanied by a telephone operator, move with the advanced element. The line back to the mortar crew is exactly two hundred yards long. One man is detailed to see that the line does not get hung on the way and as far as possible runs in a straight line. When the advanced element contacts the enemy, the observer judges the distance from himself to the target and adds the two hundred yards to the mortar range. Bracketing of fire for adjustment is considered too dangerous because of the close proximity of friend and foe.

When the Germans leave a woods or have to cross a large clearing within the wooded area, the troops work themselves close to the edge of the woods. Then all the men leave the woods simultaneously, rushing at least one hundred yards before seeking cover somewhere....."

Heavily-camouflaged German grenadiers move up into position in the Bocage country. The excellent camouflage afforded by this region has been adapted to supplement the uniforms.

Germans retreated off the Hill and myself and about twenty others managed to get right to the top, the brow of the hill, so we could overlook the German lines and we remained there for three days. We kept wondering why there was no water, food or ammunition coming to us. We had been shelled by the Tiger tanks on both sides of the orchard on top of the Hill and we got a bit fed up with this, so we thought we'd try and find softer ground to get deeper trenches. So we went round a hedge, we had been lying in a ditch by a hedge, and I said, 'hey look fellas, there's one trench here already dug for us,' so, I said, 'Before we go down, I'll fire some shots into that to make sure it's clean.' So I fired three shots from the Bren gun that I'd got with me and out came six Germans with their hands up. So we sent the prisoners back, and then behind they realised that if we'd sent prisoners back there must be somebody there, so they sent a runner and said 'what are you fellows doing here, the order to retreat was given two days ago.' We realised then why we were not getting any supplies through and why we were not getting any back up."

Also at a higher level, cooperation had been equally poor, in particular between tanks and infantry formations. Furthermore, it should be recognised that the terrain over which the attack was launched was not particularly favourable to a rapid large scale advance and also that German resistance in this area, in particular by elements of 12th SS Panzer Division, Hitler Jugend, was extremely tenacious and effective, but they did pay a high price as another veteran recalled:

"When I was on Hill 112 and we were holding back the German attacks. You know Germans are ones for precision, we knew exactly when each one was going to get up, and that's how we managed to shoot them, as they got up. We knew when they were going to get up. And of course they were doing it to precision so every time we knew when each one was going to get up and as they got up we shot them. So they retreated. A German later wrote in a book that they were not able to re-capture Hill 112 because there was a machine

gun battalion in the wood. It wasn't a machine gun battalion at all, it was us with all our Bren guns."

The arrival of large German armoured formations on the western flank of the Epsom corridor was a major threat which had to be dealt with. Nonetheless, the battle did grind to a halt in a way which was dispiriting for the British Commanders.

These Allied troops had to wait six weeks to capture the city of Caen which should had been taken on D-Day itself.

- C H A P T E R   1 3 -

OPERATION 'CHARNWOOD'

A local advance resulted in the capture of Chardonnerette, three miles north-east of Caen, on the 23rd, and during the next two days further advances were made south of Tilly sur Seulles, after hard fighting. By the 27th the British troops, including powerful armoured forces, had cut the Caen to Villers-Bocage road and railway, and reached the River Odon at a point some two miles north of Evrecy. A firm bridgehead was established and included the important high ground to the north of Esquay. German reaction to this thrust was, as expected, violent. In addition to the strong armoured forces already in the area, Panzer formations which the Germans had intended to form into a reserve were used for immediate counter-attacks, and by July 1st the greater part of eight Panzer and SS panzer divisions had been drawn into battle. The 'Epsom' attack of the British 2nd Army, commanded by Lieutenant General Sir Miles Christopher Dempsey, was a fortuitous piece of military strategy, for Rommel had hoped to be able to wait until these Panzer Divisions were fully ready, and then launch them in a concentrated attack of his own choosing.

Armoured and infantry fighting of the most bitter nature developed. The close country prevented large armoured formations being employed at single points, but the Germans put in counter-attacks of company strength, supported by tanks, at numerous points in an attempt to infiltrate into the British lines. All failed. The bridgehead remained firm and was, in fact, enlarged.

While bad weather continued to delay the planned build-up of the Allied forces, the German rate of reinforcement was affected by the activities of the French Forces of the Interior which kept considerable German forces, including Panzer Divisions, tied down in the south of France, and by the effects of the 'Transportation Plan' air attacks. The 9th SS Panzer Division, which had crossed

Germany from the eastern front in seven days, took fourteen to travel from the German frontier to the Normandy battlefield.

THE AMERICANS ATTACK

The US 1st Army, having cleared the north-west tip of the Cotentin peninsula, was now regrouped for a new drive southwards. The attack opened in a blinding rainstorm at 5.30am on July 3rd, on a wide front south of St Sauveur Le Vicomte. By the following day, the Americans had captured the tactically important high ground to the north of La Have du Puits, but enemy resistance in the town ceased only on the 9th, after it had been outflanked on the east and the west.

The next American target was to be a drive southwards to capture Avranches and St Malo along with the Breton ports of Brest and Lorient. This attack began on July 3rd and involved all three of the American corps which were stationed in the Cotentan peninsula.

Curious Allied soldiers examine the wrecked chassis of a German self-propelled gun. This is most probably a Brumbaar, a variant of the Panzer IV which was originally designed for use in the street fighting at Stalingrad.

A young German officer briefs his fellow officers in the close country of the Bocage.

Once again, however, the Bocage played its part in slowing down the American advance. For a modern mechanised army it was one of the worst types of terrain imaginable, short of jungle. By July 7th, despite having undergone four days of bitter fighting, the Americans had advanced no more than four miles.

Simultaneously, other American troops were fighting their way up the steep wooded slopes of the Forest de Mont Castre in conditions that were described as jungle warfare, but by the 11th they had reached the southern edge of the forest. The Americans also started to advance down the Carentan-Periers road, at the same time forcing a passage across the River Vire in the direction of St Jean de Daye, which fell on the 8th. By the 11th, advanced elements, pressing on through waterlogged country, were within three miles of the important communications centre of St Lô.

The British 2nd Army bridgehead across the River Orne held firm against repeated enemy counter-attacks, and on July 4th Canadian and British forces themselves attacked eastwards towards Caen.

HANDBOOK ON GERMAN MILITARY FORCES
EXTRACT NO.18
SPECIAL OPERATIONS

TOWN AND STREET FIGHTING

"....In attacking a town or village, the Germans employ flanking and encircling tactics. They attempt to cut off water, electricity, gas, and other utilities. While carrying out the flanking manoeuvre, they pin down the defenders with heavy artillery fire and aerial bombardment. When it is necessary to make a direct assault, the Germans concentrate all available heavy weapons, including artillery and air units, on one target. They favour as targets for their massed fire the forward edges of the community, especially detached groups of buildings and isolated houses. During the fire concentration the infantry assembles and attacks the objective immediately upon termination of artillery fire. Tanks and assault guns accompany the infantry, and with their fire immobilise any new enemy forces which may appear. They also support the infantry in sweeping away barricades, blasting passages through walls, and crushing wire obstacles. Guns and mortars are used against concealed positions, and antitank guns cover side streets against possible flanking operations. Machine guns engage snipers on roofs.

The immediate objective of the Germans is to divide the area occupied by the enemy. These areas then are isolated into as many smaller areas as possible, in order to deny the enemy freedom of movement.

Another form of attack employed by the Germans is to drive through a community and establish good positions beyond the town to block the retreat of the defender. Then they try to annihilate the enemy within the community.

The assaulting troops are divided into a number of columns and make a series of coordinated parallel attacks. Attacks from opposite directions and conflicting angles are avoided, since they lead to confusion and to firing on friendly troops. The columns are sub-divided into assault and mop-up groups. Assault detachments of engineers, equipped with demolition equipment, flame throwers, and grenades, accompany the infantry. Where possible, the Germans blast holes through the walls of rows of buildings along the route of advance in order to provide the infantry with covered approaches. These passages afford protection for bringing up supplies and evacuating casualties. Houses are cleared of defenders by small-arms fire. Streets are avoided as much as possible by the Germans who infiltrate simultaneously through back yards and over roofs. They attempt to further the advance by seizing high buildings which offer dominating positions and wide fields of fire.

When compelled to advance through streets, the Germans move in two files, one on each side of the thoroughfare. The

An aerial view of Caen after its liberation. Though the people who remained in the capital of Calvados throughout the fighting spoke in horror of the concentrated Allied bombing, they gave the British and Canadians an enthusiastic welcome.

left side is preferred as it is more advantageous for firing right-handed from doorways. Consideration is given to the problem of fighting against defenders organised not only in depth but in height. Consequently the men receive specific assignments to watch the rooms, the various floors of buildings, and cellar windows. Side streets are immediately blocked, and at night searchlights are kept ready to illuminate roofs.

As soon as a building is occupied, the Germans organise it into a strongpoint. Windows and other openings are converted into loopholes and embrasures. Cellars and attics are occupied first in organising for defense.

Even buildings which have been completely destroyed are kept under constant observation to prevent their re-occupation by the enemy. From occupied buildings the Germans deliver continuous machine-gun and rifle fire with the object of denying the enemy the opportunity to occupy alternate positions.

Underground corridors and sewers, which provide excellent cover for defenders, are attacked with determination. When immediate clearance or smoking-out is not possible, the entrances are barricaded, blasted, or guarded.

Aware that their tanks and assault guns are vulnerable to attacks by tank-hunting units,the Germans assign infantry to protect them. Barricades and obstacles are cleared by infantry and engineers. All able-bodied civilians, regardless of danger, are summoned to clear the streets of debris.

When a section of a town is occupied, the Germans close up all side streets leading from the occupied area, block all exits of houses, and then begin a house-to-house search with details assigned to special tasks, such as mopping up roofs, attics, basements, courtyards, and staircases....."

Intensive enemy artillery fire forced the British troops to withdraw slightly, but the Canadians, after capturing Carpiquet and part of the airfield south of the village, continued to defeat every attempt by the enemy to drive them out of their new positions. Bitter and inconclusive close quarter fighting continued for four days, which saw infantry pitted against armour.

"And then we went a little further down the road into where the railway crossed the road, the railway crossing, and four Panther tanks were being knocked out by Typhoons, they had been travelling up the railway line. We saw these four Panther tanks knocked out by Typhoons, they were really wicked these Typhoon rockets, we used to give up a cheer every time a Typhoon came when they came into the attack because we often saw them at Carpiquet Aerodrome. We were entrenched on the edge of Carpiquet Aerodrome and the Canadians were trying to capture it and they were assisted by these Typhoons with their rockets. It was fantastic, fantastic."

Early on the 8th of July, however, after a highly concentrated bombardment from heavy and medium bombers, the British and

A German Grenadier with a Panzerfaust anti-tank weapon is followed by an engineer with a flamethrower. The flamethrower was designed for use against fixed defences, and operators were particularly vulnerable in open combat.

Within days of the first landings, German prisoners were marched through the streets of England. This picture shows a column of six hundred German prisoners being marched through the suburban streets of Dover.

Canadian divisions, contained for so long by the enemy north of Caen, launched an attack which carried them to the outskirts of the town the same night. The attack was well supported by fire from massed artillery and the ships anchored off shore. By nightfall the following day, the whole town except for suburbs south of the River Orne had been taken, and small pockets in the rear were being rapidly eliminated, while the Canadians at last completed their capture of Carpiquet aerodrome.

By the 15th, the US 1st Army was within sight of Lessay, Periers, and St Lô. At the same time the American advance down the Carentan-Periers road and the widening of the bridgehead made earlier across the River Vire, resulted in a straightening of the general line and the elimination of resistance in the flooded areas south of Carentan. To the east of St Lô, further steady gains were made between the 11th and 13th, including the cutting of the St Lô-Berigny road. The town of St Lô fell on July 18th after eight days' fierce fighting.

- C H A P T E R   1 4 -

OPERATION 'GOODWOOD'

Following the capture of the northern part of Caen and the expansion eastwards of the Odon bridgehead, the British 2nd Army paused for regrouping before launching an attack at dusk on July 15th on the line Noyers-Bougy-Esquay. Good progress was made against stiff resistance, but the main achievement of the attack, whether intended or accidental, was that it held a considerable part of the Germany armour west of the Orne, where it became heavily involved with consequent losses.

Then at 8.45am on the 18th, General Montgomery attacked again with powerful forces of infantry and armour south-east of Caen. The assault was preceded by the heaviest and most concentrated bombing undertaken to that date in support of military operations. Over two thousand British and American heavy and medium bombers, (of which only nine were lost), dropped 7,000 to 8,000 tons of bombs in an area of little more than seventy square miles, blasting a seven thousand yard wide passage between the suburb of Vaucelles and the woods of Touffreville and Cagny. Armoured formations then crossed the River Orne by specially constructed bridges and, through the gap made by the bombers, drove strong wedges in the direction of Cagny and Bourguebus. Despite the initial success of the thrust by British armour to the east of Caen, the German defensive positions, and in particular the very heavy anti-tank screens to the south and east of Bourguebus, halted the advance with considerable losses on both sides. By the afternoon of the first day of the assault, the momentum of the drive was slowing down in the face of this powerful opposition, and a pause was made to allow the infantry to come up.

On the next day violent rainstorms so softened the ground that no movement was possible off metalled roads. Meanwhile, Canadian

OPERATION GOODWOOD

With half of Caen already in British hands, Operation Goodwood was designed to expand on the gains and provide the jumping off point for a series of future attacks. The Canadian armoured forces attacked to the west of Caen, where they encountered stiff resistance from the first SS Panzer Corps. To the east of the city, the remnants of the 21st Panzer Division were pushed back by a combined Canadian and British advance. Despite the fact that the operation is often cited as a failure, by the end of the battle the British and Canadians were firmly in control of Caen and had expanded the frontline to a depth of ten miles south of the city.

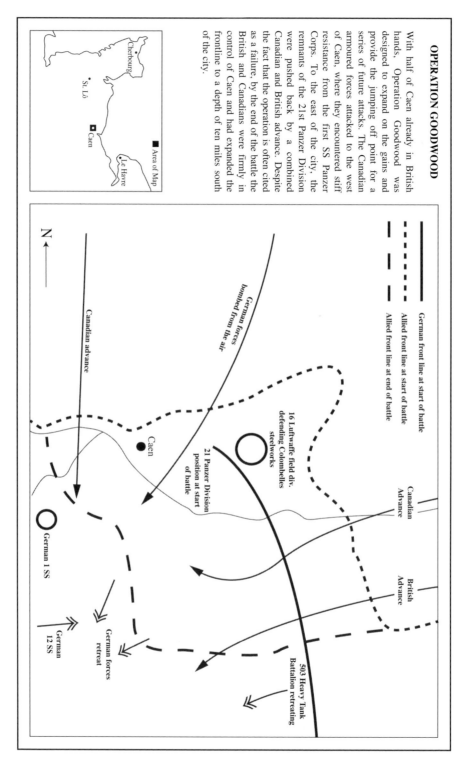

Cherbourg

St. Lô

Caen

Le Havre

■ Area of Map

N →

German front line at start of battle

Allied front line at start of battle

Allied front line at end of battle

German forces bombed from the air

Canadian advance

16 Luftwaffe field div. defending Colombelles steelworks

21 Panzer Division position at start of battle

Caen

Canadian Advance

British Advance

503 Heavy Tank Battalion retreating

German 1 SS

German forces retreat

German 12 SS

With briefcases and well-nourished frames, these German officers from a coastal garrison are surrendering to the Allies.

troops had successfully cleared the southern and south-eastern suburbs of Caen, and British infantry had thrust out towards Troarn, clearing several fortified villages. A further Canadian attack across the Orne, west of Caen, resulted in the capture of Fleury and the clearing of the east bank of the river for some three miles due south.

Operation 'Goodwood' is perhaps the most controversial of all of Montgomery's battles during the Normandy campaign. Measuring its success or failure really depends on what one chooses to believe Operation Goodwood was intended to achieve. If, for example, one believes what some historians argue, that the attack was supposed to be a breakthrough attack then, quite clearly, it failed to achieve its objectives. If, however, one accepts that Operation 'Goodwood' was supposed to pin German formations, in particular Panzer formations, opposite the British sector, so that the American breakthrough attempt would be more likely to succeed when it was launched, the judgement has to be rather more favourable.

It is also worth bearing in mind that Operation 'Goodwood' did result in the clearing of thirty square miles of territory from which the later British and Canadian offensives were successfully launched. Although the losses were heavy (six thousand personnel had been killed or wounded including the parallel Canadian Operation 'Atlantic' which took place at the same time as 'Goodwood', and five hundred tanks had been destroyed), the British controlled the battlefield at the end of 'Goodwood'. As a result, well over two hundred of the lost tanks were in fact recovered and put back into action. Finally, the success of Operation Goodwood needs to be viewed in terms of the effects on German morale.

On 21st July, one day after Operation 'Goodwood' terminated, Field Marshal von Kluge, the new German commander in the west, wrote a letter to Hitler which said that the war was lost, and the chronological coincidence would suggest that the end of 'Goodwood' and the writing of the letter was no accident.

An Allied Sherman passes American infantry standing amidst the wreckage of German armour. The numbered object in the foreground is the turret of a German tank, which has been completely blown off the chassis and turned upside down. The vehicle in the background appears to be a Tiger Mark One.

- C H A P T E R   1 5 -

THE JULY PLOT

The successes which the Allies won after June 6th threw the Goebbels machine into some confusion. Prophecies that the Anglo-American army would soon be wholly destroyed were intermixed with warnings about the material superiority of the Allies whose forces Eisenhower allegedly threw into the battle, *"without any regard for the frightful sacrifice in human lives."* After the fall of Cherbourg and the conquest of the whole Cotentin Peninsula, even German propaganda could not pretend that the Allies would be thrown back into the sea. Under the stress of the declining situation in Normandy, those army circles which had, for many months, been secretly planning the overthrow of the Hitler regime, at last felt themselves compelled to act. The full story will never be known, as the Nazis, naturally, distorted the reports to suit their own needs. The plot itself had been worked out in complete secrecy by a limited number of high ranking army officers. The general plan was to get rid of Hitler, (thus freeing the Army from its military oath), to seize all the command centres in Berlin and the main cities of the Reich, to arrest the most important Nazi officials, and to disarm the SS. The moment for the revolt, several times postponed, had been fixed for October, by which time it was expected that the climax of the war would have been reached and all preparations would have been completed. As a result of the declining situation on both fronts the date was advanced by about three months, with the result that the venture was at least in part improvised, and this contributed to its failure.

The inner circle of the conspirators consisted almost exclusively of officers who belonged, or had previously belonged, to the German General Staff. Highest in rank was Field-Marshal von Witzleben. Beside him stood several Colonel-Generals, among them two who had previously held the office of Chief of the General Staff: Beck, a man of the highest ability, who had retired after the invasion of Austria, and his successor Halder. The Chief of Staff at the time, General Zeitzler, seems also to have directly participated.

Three men had a particularly important role to play: General Olbrecht, Quartermaster-General of the Army, Colonel-General Fromm, Commander-in-Chief of the Home Army, (Heimatheer), and therefore of almost all troops in Inner Germany, and Colonel-General Hoeppner. Olbrecht was, with Beck, the main driving force of the revolt, and his ADC, Colonel von Stauffenberg, was chosen to start the whole movement by eliminating Hitler. On July 20th, Stauffenberg went to the Fuhrer's headquarters carrying a small time-bomb which he had carried in a yellow briefcase. He entered the room where a conference was held in Hitler's presence, put the briefcase down then made an excuse and left. The room had been expected by the conspirators to be an underground room with concrete walls which would withstand and throw back the blast, killing whoever was standing or sitting anywhere near the exploding bomb. Actually, the conference took place in a wooden hut the walls

Hitler and Mussolini meet with various party officials in the aftermath of the July plot.

of which collapsed easily. Hitler, at the moment of the explosion, had just moved from the table under which the bomb had been deposited. Thus he was not killed but suffered only slight bruises.

Stauffenberg, however, who had managed to leave the hut a few minutes before the explosion was due, saw, or at least heard, the explosion. He at once boarded a plane for Berlin, certain that Hitler was dead. Everything now depended on the speed and resolution of the main actors in Berlin. It was only by perfect co-ordination and quick action that there could be any hope of forestalling the countermoves which were certain to come from the Party. The key to all further moves was in the hands of the Commander-in-Chief of the Home Army, General Fromm.

The conspirators were masters of the War Ministry at the Bendlerstrasse, the centre and brain of the German military machine. All outgoing orders as well as incoming inquiries had to go through the teleprinting office there. When Stauffenberg arrived with the news that Hitler was killed, the conspirators asked Fromm to give the orders necessary to secure Berlin and the main centres outside the capital. Some of these orders were given, but then Fromm suddenly lost his nerve and collapsed. Stauffenberg tried to take over, but being only a colonel, met resistance from many officers in the War Ministry who might have obeyed Fromm. Colonel General Beck, who tried to strengthen Stauffenberg's hand, had not sufficient authority, having been long in retirement. An open struggle ensued, and Beck and Stauffenberg were captured after a fight with revolvers.

Although people in Berlin perceived little of what was happening, it was not until the evening that the Nazis were again in full control of the military machine, and that communication with Hitler was restored. In Hamburg, Munich and Vienna, the three most important places outside Berlin, the commanding officers received the first orders given by Fromm and acted accordingly. They told their officers that Hitler was dead and that they were no longer bound by the oath on his name. State and Party buildings were occupied, and in some places fierce fighting started between Army and SS units. These movements collapsed only after it was generally realised that Hitler was alive, and that the capital was under Party control.

In Vienna, the revolt continued throughout most of July 21st. High Party and Gestapo officials were arrested. Army units participated, and the Austrian underground movement, led in Vienna by Socialist and Communist workers, came into the open. Workers with armlets of the People's Guards protected some of the main buildings as well as foreign consulates.

To the Nazis all this was a godsend. They had had many suspicions. But what all the work of the Gestapo had not been able to provide was now presented to them gratuitously, a long list of their enemies, from left to right throughout 'Greater Germany'.

They took frightful vengeance. They put up a 'Court of Honour of the German Army', asking Field-Marshal von Rundstedt, now retired from his command in Normandy, to preside over it. There is nothing to show that Rundstedt was one of the conspirators, but there is little doubt that, had they won, Rundstedt would have been prepared to collaborate with them. He was the most successful,

Winston Churchill visits Caen in the aftermath of its capture.

the most experienced and in many ways, the most respected of all German Army commanders. Had he refused to preside over that court, he would have shown that he approved of what the conspirators had done and would have been executed himself. But by making him the instrument of their vengeance, and the hangman of his comrades, the Nazis insured that the Army could never trust him as a possible leader against the Party,

After the 'Court of Honour' had delivered all the accused officers, with Field-Marshal von Witzleben at the top, to the People's Court- because, "by their deeds they had put themselves outside the ranks of the German Army", that Court, presided over by the notorious Roland Freissler, quickly sentenced them all to death. Gallows were erected on big motor lorries, and after the accused had been hanged, the lorries with their horrible load went in slow procession through the streets of Berlin, so as to show everyone that even a German Field Marshal, a man considered a demi-god in old Prussia or the Kaiser's Germany, had to die this shameful death if he dared to conspire against the holy person of the Fuhrer. The relatives of the executed were forced to follow the gallows, and most of them were killed immediately afterwards. Whole families were murdered, in some cases down to children of four and five years old.

The mass killing continued throughout the year. As a matter of course, not only every officer and soldier, but anybody else who could be suspected of having had anything to do with the attempted plot was put to death. Most of the victims were kept imprisoned and were tortured by the Gestapo in order to make them reveal their connections and accomplices. (Fifteen hundred officers were arrested during the first few days after the revolt.)

Nor was that enough. This time the Nazi leaders were resolved to get rid, not only of those who had had anything to do with the events of July 20th, but also of all potential enemies of the regime capable of exerting any influence. It was no more coincidence that the second group of people condemned to death by the People's Court were not tried in public, as Witzleben and his comrades had

German vehicles and armour destroyed from the air by Allied fighter bombers. The vehicle in the foreground is a Kubelwagen, a general purpose vehicle.

been. This second group consisted almost entirely of well known politicians of the Weimar Republic, drawn from all parties, from the Social Democrats to the German Nationalists. There were also some professional diplomats, among them the former ambassador in Rome, von Hassell. Without having been let into the secret of the time and place of the planned attempt on Hitler's life, some of these civilians had nevertheless been in contact with the conspirators. A connection confirmed when, in July 1945, the Bishop of Chichester, the Right Reverend G.K.A. Bell, made public information he had received for transmission to the British Government while he was in Sweden in May 1942. At that time, more than two years before the attempt, a German pastor, Dietrich Bonhoeffer, told him of the plot and the names of the people involved in it. A few of these civilians had probably been selected as possible members of the mainly military government which it had been intended to set up. Others, however, were considered by the Nazis to be potential enemies of the regime, who might have been prepared to join any successful rising, and the Nazis put them all to death.

On the other hand, the Nazis were most anxious to prove to the German people that, as Hitler put it in a hurried speech, "only a very small clique" of generals had taken part in the plot. They maintained that no one in a really responsible position had had anything to do with it, and they therefore had to suppress a number of the most important names. They did not mention Fromm, nor Zeitzler, whose name was not heard again after the announcement that Zeitzler was, "suffering from an infectious disease and could not carry out his duties for some weeks." Guderian had taken over the office of Chief of Staff. It is now well known that the circumstantial reports given out of Field Marshal Rommel's having suffered head injuries owing to a car accident due to an air attack, and having died in consequence, were lies. Rommel's end was announced on October 15th, but rumours that he was dead had swept through the German army many weeks before that date. He had certainly at least given his blessing to the revolt, and all the tales about his wounds seem to have been designed to cover up the fact that Germany's most popular commander and Hitler's special favourite had made common cause with his enemies and shared their fate.

The exact number of people murdered by the Gestapo during the months following July 20th will never be known, but they certainly amounted to tens of thousands. They ranged from hundreds of members of old, influential 'society' families in Berlin and elsewhere (always including women, often children), to thousands of political prisoners in concentration camps, thousands of workers in Berlin, Munich, Vienna, Hamburg and western Germany, (including a high percentage of the old leaders and officials of trade unions, whether Socialist or Roman Catholic). It was a mortal blow struck at every group which might have leanings in opposition to the regime and might supply the basis of a resistance movement before the final military collapse of Germany.

The destruction of all potential resistance was, however, only one of the benefits the Nazi regime derived from the events of July 20th. There was also the legend of Hitler's miraculous escape. The

Fuhrer, destined to 'save Germany' clearly had 'a charmed life.' Hardly less important in Nazi eyes, was the fact that a new 'stab-in-the-back' legend had been secured. In 1918 it was alleged that the German Army, 'undefeated in the field', had been stabbed in the back by 'Marxist defeatists and traitors.' This time the Party charged the 'traitors in the Army' with having stabbed the fighting German people in the back. It was said that the treacherous generals had held back reserve troops, and so caused the breakdown of the Eastern front.

On July 24th it was announced from Hitler's headquarters that, at the request of all parts of the armed forces, the Hitler salute with the greeting, "Heil Hitler", would be substituted for the military salute. Much more important was an order by which professional soldiers, including the whole officers' corps, were allowed to join the Nazi Party, whereas previously any association with political bodies had been prohibited.

With the Allied domination of the air, a number of attempts were made to produce decoys - in this case a wooden model of a Panther tank has been constructed.

Hermann Goering inspects the damage in the aftermath of the explosion. Hitler's life was saved by the heavy oak table which absorbed the full force of the blast.

- CHAPTER 16 -

OPERATION 'COBRA'

By July 15th, in exchange for ten thousand casualties, the Americans had progressed only seven miles from their start point. With both the British and the Americans now encountering savage resistance, it was agreed at a conference attended by Sir Bernard Montgomery and Omar Bradley, that a new operation, code named 'Cobra' would be put into affect. 'Cobra' was to result in the entrapment of the German forces in Normandy in a huge pocket, which would ultimately be centred on the town of Falaise.

In the meantime, US casualties continued to grow and by July 23rd they had suffered more than forty thousand casualties in the fighting, which began to place a severe strain on the replacement system. One major advantage for the American troops, however, was that the British troops were performing the task of tying down the bulk of the German armoured formations. Six Panzer divisions were tied down around Caen, while only two under strength Panzer divisions opposed the US troops. Despite the casualties and the blood- shed, the time was now ripe for the break out into the open.

The American cause was further helped by the fact that on July 1st, Field Marshal von Runstedt, who had been accused by Hitler of defeatism, could take no more and resigned his post as Commander in the West. Shortly afterwards Field Marshal Erwin Rommel was badly injured when his car was struck by a British fighter bomber. As we have seen, Hitler's confidence in his army was finally shattered by the bomb plot of July 20th, after which Hitler completely distrusted all of his army commanders and had refused them any real ability to control the battle.

The Fuhrer was now effectively attempting to micromanage three massive campaigns, on three separate fronts. The only likely outcome was disaster. To make matters worse the recovering

OPERATION COBRA

With American forces now in control of the entire Cherbourg peninsula, significant US armoured elements were able to slip into the interior of France through the Avranches Gap and begin to capture the Brittany ports. The initial plan had called for what Montgomery described as the "long hook", which was originally designed to entrap the German forces in a vast encircling movement. As the situation developed, however, it became obvious that the ill-conceived counter-attack at Mortain had produced the circumstances which could lead to the capture or destruction of Germany's effective fighting force at the pocket of Falaise.

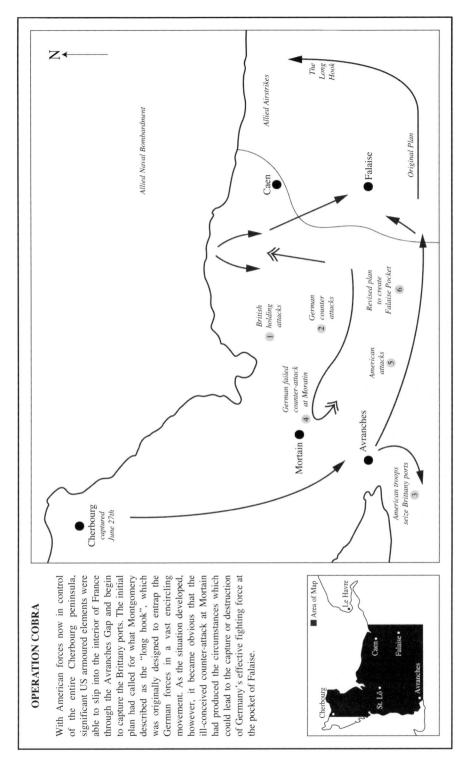

In the protective wake of a Sherman tank, British troops move forward to the attack in Normandy.

A powerful demonstration of the destructive capacity of Allied air power. This jumble of wreckage represents the vehicles of a German division which were caught by the bombs of Allied heavy bombers at Rouen Docks, as the German forces desperately tried to find a route over the Seine.

Rommel was implicated in the July plot, and faced with the threat of retribution against his family, took the option of suicide.

Initially, Operation 'Cobra' made little progress. There was still the remnant of the Bocage country to be cleared, but once more the massive supremacy of the Allied airforce began to pay dividends. More than 500 tonnes of high explosives were dropped on the German defences. The newly arrived von Kluge from the Eastern Front, was convinced that the real break out would naturally take place from the British sector and refused to send precious reinforcements to replace the losses. So on July 26th, American tanks finally smashed through the German defences and broke into the open country beyond. They had finally left the Bocage behind them and now dashed headlong into the interior of France. It was now that the famous US Commander General George Patton, sprang into action. Patton had already seen action in Tunisia and had led the US 7th Army in Sicily. At last the Allies had the situation that suited them, mobile warfare in open country, which suited the highly mechanised American forces. More and more US troops now poured through the Avranches gap and raced into the interior of France. The first objectives were the Brittany ports. German defence of the ports in Brittany proved to be tenacious. St Malo did not fall to the American forces until August 16th. Brest held out for even longer - until September 18th - and in one of the little known facts of the war both Lorient and St Nazaire were held in German hands until the war ended. The Germans were besieged like garrisons of a medieval castle, but nonetheless, it is true to say that the whole of France was never liberated.

A rear view of a Tiger I. This was the most vulnerable area of the tank and was frequently the only option for Allied tanks who had found that the Tiger's frontal armour was almost impervious to many of their anti-tank weapons.

The distorted mass of pipe work inside this German locomotive has been twisted into a curious flower shape by the force of a direct hit from an Allied fighter bomber.

THE AMERICANS BREAK THROUGH

A week after the British 2nd Army's 'Goodwood' offensive and just five days after the July plot, the US 1st Army achieved a spectacular breakthrough. The attack, code-named Operation 'Cobra', which began west of St Lô on July 25th, made rapid progress, Marigny and St Gilles, lying seven and four miles west of St Lô respectively, being captured on the following morning. The attacking force, which included a large proportion of armour, then fanned out into three columns, directed west, south and south-west. The first was within five miles of Coutances by the 27th, while another, after capturing Canisy, (27th), swung west and reached a point ten miles north-east of Granville on the 29th. By the same date the third column was within seven miles of Villedieu. On the extreme right flank Lessay and Periers fell on the 27th. An armoured column thrusting down the Periers-Coutances road occupied Coutances on July 28th, there joining American forces advancing from the east.

Next day the sea was reached south of the Seine estuary, and during that afternoon the tempo of the advance increased. By nightfall of the 30th American armour swept through Brehal, and on the 31st reached and captured Avranches and Granville. Farther east US forces captured Berigny on July 27th and straightened out the enemy salient south of the town on the 28th.

THE BRITISH ATTACK

Two important attacks in the British sector contributed to the success of the American operations farther west. The first was launched on July 25th by the Canadians down the Caen-Falaise road. Although

Troops of the American 3rd Army, advancing from Le Mans, reached the Argentan area on August 12th, 1944, but it was not until some days later that they made contact with British and Canadian troops closing in from the north on the Germans trapped in the 'Falaise Gap.'

almost no ground was won, owing to repeated and furious counter-attacks, the attack succeeded in containing the great bulk of the enemy armour at the vital moment of the American breakthrough. The centre of activity of the second was the area of Caumont, where British troops had secretly taken over from the Americans. A British armoured and infantry force made a major attack on the 30th, after a heavy preliminary air bombardment, and by August 1st had secured Cahagnes and Le Beny Bocage. The next two days saw a further expansion of the initial assault towards Vire, Aunay sur Odon and Villers-Bocage, and by the 4th the outskirts of all three villages had been reached. The much disputed villages of Evrecy and Esquay, south-west of Caen, were captured on August 4th, and the ruined Villers-Bocage fell to the British on August 5th.

CHAPTER 17

THE MORTAIN COUNTER-ATTACK

On June 25, SHAEF announced that General Joseph Koenig, Commander in Chief of the French forces in Britain, had been vested by the French National Committee with the command of the French Forces of the Interior, acting under the direction of the Supreme Commander. In Brittany, the FFI now seized high ground in advance of the thrusts by American armour and also engaged in guerrilla warfare, to harass the Germans and to protect Allied lines of communication. Elsewhere in France, they blew up bridges, put locomotives out of action, derailed trains, and cut the underground long-distance cable between Paris and Berlin.

During the first days of August, the speed of the American advance into the Brittany peninsula resulted in a fluid front. One armoured column, pushing southwards and westwards, reached the area of Dinan on the 3rd, turned south and then altered direction towards Brest, liberating several Breton towns en route. Another column liberated Rennes, capital of Brittany, virtually intact on the 4th and, advancing southwest, reached the River Vilaine on the 6th, thus sealing off the Brittany peninsula. An American column liberated Vannes, (6th), and began to close in on Lorient on the 8th. Meanwhile US infantry had attacked St Malo, the citadel of which did not surrender till the 17th. Other forces moved south, reaching Nantes and Angers on the 9th. Patrols crossed the Loire on the 11th.

Bradley saw the danger of Patton sitting down to a series of sieges and in a masterful assessment of the overall situation urged Patton to strike first south and then east to begin to close what was later to be the Falaise pocket. In order to link to the US forces, the British Second Army was now driving south towards the town of Vire, but once again the deadly Bocage country had conspired to

MORTAIN COUNTER-ATTACK

The counter-attack at Mortain ranks as a spectacularly ill-conceived effort to prevent the US troops from advancing through the Avranches Gap. By cutting off the Cherbourg peninsula, Hitler had hoped to bottle up the US forces and prevent them exploiting the break-through into the interior, but by relieving the pressure on Montgomery's British and Canadian forces, he set up the circumstances for the disaster which would befall the German forces at Falaise.

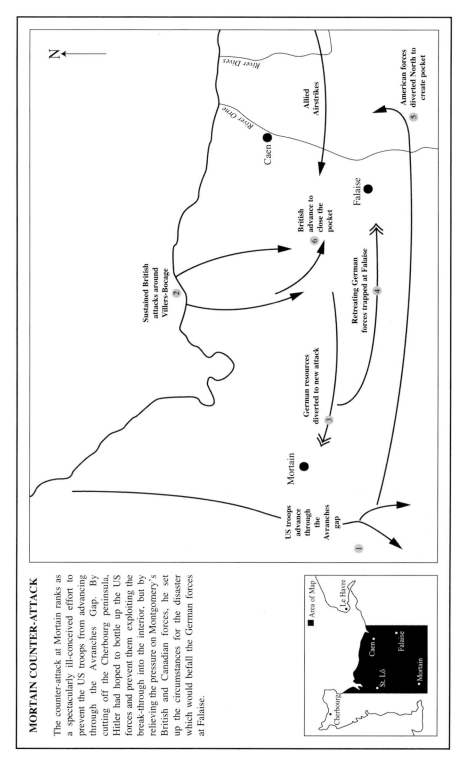

interfere with the campaign which was continuing to drain British casualties at First World War rates of attrition.

Two further large operations mainly involving Canadian forces were staged in August. Although Operation Totalise could not be deemed a success, Operation Tractable, the action which followed enjoyed a far better outcome as the hard pressed German forces were further ground down. One highly disconcerting factor was the large number of self-inflicted casualties sustained by the Allies, in particular this was due to what was known as short bombings, the massive Allied bombing formations, dropped their bombs short of the target. This was blamed on a lack of co-ordination between the ground and air forces. One particularly depressing instance was that the Canadians used yellow smoke to mark their lines, while the bombers were using yellow smoke as a target indicator. The problems on the ground were compounded by Montgomery's lack of faith in the Canadian Commander, Clara.

A wrecked German half-track from an SS division lies on its side next to one of its fallen occupants. The American soldier is standing aboard a Wespe, one of the new breed of German self-propelled artillery which provided effective fire support for the Panzer divisions. They were , however, never available in adequate numbers; only 635 of these very useful vehicles were produced to satisfy the unceasing demands of both the Western and Eastern fronts.

A vivid image of the destructive power wrought by Allied air forces in the confined spaces of the Normandy lanes.

At the eastern end of the American sector a large area of country was cleared between Villedieu and Vire, and, while fighting was still proceeding in Mortain, advanced elements pushed on beyond Barenton. On the nights of August 6th to 7th, however, the Germans made a powerful counter-attack westward from the Mortain area, near the junction of the American and British fronts, and aimed at splitting the Allies by cutting through the bottleneck at Avranches.

The German armour was contributing strongly to the defence around Caen. Amazingly, the six Panzer divisions serving against the British and Canadian forces had managed to keep at least half of their tanks in action, and these excellent machines were making the advance very difficult. It was at this point that Hitler decided to intervene personally in the battle, and this intervention was to have disastrous consequences. He ordered that all of the available Panzer units on the Normandy front were to be sent into a concerted attack against the Americans. This attack was to be centred on the town of Mortain situated to the east of Avranches. His intention was to close the Avranches bottleneck, through which the American troops were slipping into the interior, thus isolating Patton's forces from the rest of the Allied forces. While the plan had some appeal in logic, in practice it was an impossible scheme.

Von Kluge in particular was thunder struck. The tanks had been fighting superbly in their defensive role but the problems of supply in particular and the lack of German resources, meant that a counter attack really was out of the question. Nonetheless, one hundred tanks under General Hans von Luck were hastily assembled and in an ill-prepared assault struck against Mortain. To confound matters, the Americans had de-coded German signals and massive Allied air strikes disrupted the German thrust, destroying many of the tanks.

With the support of tankbuster aircraft, the Americans met, checked and held this attack, which was carried out by elements of four Panzer divisions. Counter-attacking, they prevented the enemy from disengaging while the jaws of a trap were closing between Argentan and Falaise.

SHERMAN 'FIREFLY'

The Sherman M4 was the workhorse of the Allied armies in Normandy. The superior numbers of these vehicles were often used to overcome the qualitative advantages which the German tanks, such as the Tiger and the Panther, enjoyed. One successful development was the mounting of a 17lb high velocity anti-tank gun which proved to be much more efficient in the battlefield. This new variant was known as the 'Firefly'.

FALAISE

Throughout July, the British and Canadians had continued to pound steadily against the strongest defences yet encountered in northern France. Although no dramatic results were achieved, their contribution to the outcome of the first phase of the Battle of France should not be underestimated. The opening actions which led to the Falaise pocket were to be Gordon Mucklow's last battle.

"We never thought to be scared, you had a job to do, and you got on and did it. It was only afterwards when you realised what you had done. The next action was for capturing Manpassant and that's the beginning of the closing of the Falaise gap. We had to take the Ridge. Everywhere we went we marched, but on this occasion we realised there was going to be some big battle, because we were given transport; we clung to Sherman tanks and they took us to the start line of the attack. We made the attack on the Ridge and as I approached the summit of the Ridge there was a captain from the Somerset Light Infantry. He put me in charge of the Piat team, which was myself and a firer, a loader and two carrying projectiles, and by the time we got to the top there was only me with the Piat and one fellow carrying projectiles. A sergeant ran over to us and said, 'There is a tank warning, Corporal, you can take the tank that is coming up the centre, I will take the one on the left flank, and the Sergeant Major will take the one on the right flank.' So off they went their various ways and left me on the top of this hill and I found a good position in a rut where the farm carts had gone in and out of the gate. The ruts were nice and deep so I was able to get in the rut with the Piat, waiting for my tank to appear. A Tiger tank duly appeared and he decided to then let go with his big gun, and I later learned from the Germans themselves that it was in fact a 88mm gun, it was a huge thing and I was looking straight down the barrel

THE FALAISE POCKET

In the wake of the disastrous counter-attack at Mortain, the remaining German forces now found themselves at the mercy of overwhelming Allied superiority on the ground, and more importantly, in the air. With two major river barriers to cross, the German forces which sought to escape from the Falaise pocket were forced to abandon almost all of their heavy equipment, and make their escape on foot. By the end of the battle, German forces in Normandy had effectively ceased to exist as a fighting force. The allies counted over 550 tanks, 1000 artillery pieces and 7,700 wrecked vehicles in the scattered debris of the Bocage country. Between 20,000 and 40,000 Germans had managed to escape, but 50,000 stayed behind as prisoners and 10,000 were killed.

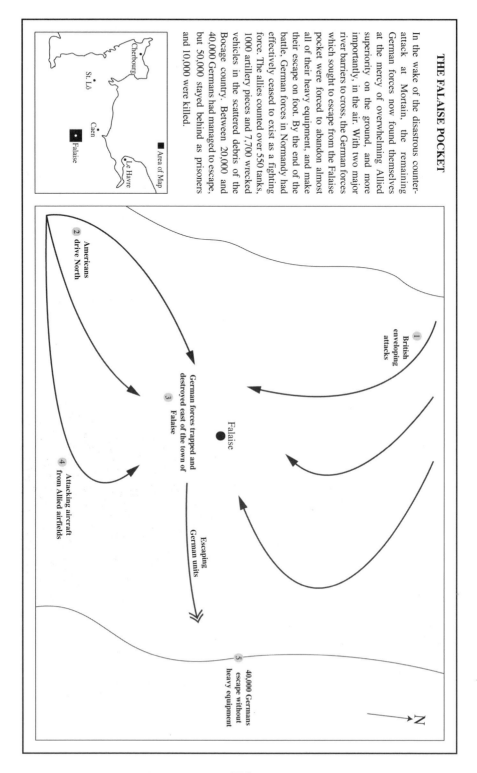

■ Area of Map

Cherbourg

St. Lô

Caen

Falaise

Le Havre

1 British enveloping attacks

2 Americans drive North

Falaise

3 German forces trapped and destroyed east of the town of Falaise

4 Attacking aircraft from Allied airfields

Escaping German units

5 40,000 Germans escape without heavy equipment

N

276

of it. So I was hit all down the left side from my head down to my shoulder and of course my hand was on the Piat so I caught it on the hand. The shrapnel went straight through my wrist in one side and came out the other and I had shrapnel in the hand and then all the way down the side of my face. I then walked down to the base of the hill to the first field dressing station with my hand on my tin hat, and I had wound my arm up to try and stop the blood oozing out, When I got to the first field dressing station I kept saying, 'Do something with my arm. It's my arm that's hurting.' They said, 'No it isn't, it's your face.' They bound my face up, by that time I went blind and they told me afterwards that was from the flash from the Tiger tank. I was blind for about two days."

On the night of August 6th, the British left flank crossed the River Orne some two and a half miles north of Thury Harcourt. This bridgehead, which was the scene of hard fighting to retain a footing, was steadily expanded. A German salient between the British and Canadian forces was eliminated on the 12th. Canadian and

Dead men and wrecked material litter the narrow lanes of the German route of escape in the Falaise pocket.

The British Piat anti-tank weapon. This was by no means as effective as the Panzerfaust and really needed to be wielded against German armour from the side or the rear to produce a kill.

British troops of the 1st Canadian Army had meanwhile attacked southwards at 11.30pm on the 7th from their Caen positions. The Canadians, pushing steadily on, were within a mile of Falaise by the 15th. Progress was also made due east of Caen, in the direction of Lisieux. Other British troops, fighting their way south through close and difficult country reached Flers and Conde sur Noireau.

With British, Canadians and Polish Armoured Divisions steadily advancing from the north and Americans, (including the French 2nd Armoured Division), closing in from the west and south, a large part of the German 7th Army was almost surrounded. It only remained to close the narrow Falaise-Argentan gap to cut the enemy's last escape route. This move was achieved by the Americans who, advancing from Le Mans with great weight behind them, reached the Argentan area on August 12th. It was the French Armoured Division, under the command of the Americans, which came close to sealing the pocket when they met the Canadians at Chambois, south of Falaise, on the

19th. The enemy had been making frantic attempts to extricate his trapped forces through the narrowing gap, and the Allied air forces had taken full advantage of such a magnificent target.

"We watched one of the biggest air-raids that were ever made on the Falaise forest. At night time it was a continuous artillery barrage, bombing, shelling this forest and in daytime I looked outside about six in the morning and in the distance it looked just like a lot of crows coming towards us. There were absolutely hundreds and hundreds of four and two engined bombers and fighter escorts coming over and we stood and watched the bombs drop out and this went on for twelve hours continually. The amazing thing is that some of the Germans survived. How, I will never know".

The Allied plans for the battles in Normandy had revolved around what Montgomery described as the 'Long Hook', while the Third Army blockaded the gap between Paris and Orleans, between the lower Loire and La Seine. The British would swing left from Falaise across the Seine. This was designed to entrap the entire surviving German forces in the West in the grasp of a huge Allied

Germans captured at Cherbourg.

Allied troops sift through the wreckage of a German supply column destroyed from the air as it retreated through the Falaise gap. In the foreground are the remains of a German half track and a motor cycle.

The German armies which took to the field in Normandy included over one million men, supported by over 1500 tanks and some 3500 guns. This vast assemblage needed over 20,000 vehicles and 20,000 horses.

By the end of the campaign, the Germans had lost some 240,000 men killed and wounded, a further 200,000 as prisoners of war and practically all of the tanks, guns and vehicles. In that respect, the battle for Normandy must rank as a strategic victory on a par with the destruction of the Army Group Centre, the outcome of Operation Bagration which was taking place in Russia, at the same time. Taken Together these two campaigns represent the decisive blows from which there was no possible prospect of recovery.

encirclement. But as the situation continued to develop Eisenhower telephoned Montgomery on the afternoon of the 8th of August to discuss the American plan, which became known as the 'Short Hook', under which the US Third Army along with Canadians and the British would meet south of Argentan to create a smaller pocket, but which was designed to capture up to sixty thousand German troops. Montgomery was receptive to the idea, and the plans were quickly changed to make provision for the 'Short Hook' with the view to closing the trap near to Argentan.

It was now that the Allied strategy began to pay dividends. Patton's forces of the Third Army now began to swing North from Le Mans towards Argentan, where they hoped to link up with the Anglo-Canadian forces attacking south from Caen, in order to create a huge pocket at Falaise. Actually the pocket around Falaise was never fully closed and a large number of German troops did manage to escape. The congestion was such that the slow moving columns of Germans were desperately exposed to the massive Allied air and ground superiority. The constricting boundaries of the pocket as they shrank, eventually were confined to an area of seven miles by seven miles, which was closed on three sides. Through the small seven-mile gap the German forces were pounded mercilessly as they tried to escape.

Intensive fighting continued inside the pocket, and on the 20th, by sustained counter-attacks, the Germans succeeded in forcing a small break in the Allied line through which a portion of their armour escaped. But the gap which was small was resealed. Terrible slaughter was inflicted on the enemy in and around the village of St Lambert where, as the war office correspondents recalled: *"German life had ceased with tragic and terrible suddenness. Dead choked the village street and surrounding meadows. By August 22nd the disorganised remnants of von Kluge's 7th Army had been taken prisoner and the pocket eliminated."*

Ten thousand German troops died as they tried desperately to escape from the Falaise pocket. Another fifty thousand were taken prisoner, which meant that the German forces in Normandy had effectively been destroyed. Of fifty divisions, forty had been wiped from the German order of battle. In addition every single Tiger tank fighting in the west had been destroyed, along with the bulk of the German armoured forces. The German industrial network was no longer capable of replacing these machines, and it was now obvious that the end of the war had been brought into sight.

Although many historians have since disputed the veracity of the following statements, the contemporary view was that the campaign had gone to plan.

Perhaps the last word should go to Sir James Grigg who, in his capacity of Secretary of State for War, was certainly a Montgomery believer. His view was firmly with the school of thought that the whole campaign went to a plan and in 1945 in his speech to the

One year after the fighting on the beaches for Normandy, German P.O.W's tend the cemetery which houses the graves of the American servicemen who fell on Utah beach.

House of Commons he presented his argument for subscribing to that view:

"Few campaigns can ever have gone more 'according to plan' than that of June, July and August, 1944. I remember being present, a month or six weeks before D-Day, at a conference where the Land, Sea and Air Commanders expounded their plans, and gave out their provisional orders. At the end of his exposition, Field Marshal (then General) Montgomery put on the wall a large map showing where he expected the Anglo-Canadian-American forces to be at D+90. Somewhere about D+80, I was visiting the General at his field HQ. The dispositions of the Allied Forces were almost exactly as they had appeared on the map I saw at the preview, but the position of the Germans was quite different. They had stood and fought on the wrong side of the Seine, a great part of them had been destroyed in consequence, and the way was open for a rapid advance beyond the Seine to the very German border."

SELECT BIBLIOGRAPHY

- Agte, Patrick. Michael Wittman. J.J. Fedorowicz Pub Inc. Canada. 1996.
- Ambrose, Stephen. The Supreme Commander. New York. 1970.
- Aron, Robert. De Gaulle Before Paris. New York. 1962.
- Aron, Robert. De Gaulle Triumphant. New York. 1964.
- Batchelor & Hogg. Artillery. New York. 1973.
- Bauer, Lt.Col Eddy. The History of World War II. Orbis Publishing Ltd. London. 1983.
- Belchem, David. All in a Day's March. London. 1967.
- Belchem, David. Victory In Normandy. London. 1981.
- Belfield, Eversley & Essame, H. The Battle for Normandy. Batsford Ltd. 1965.
- Bennett, Ralph. Ultra in the West, The Normandy Campaign. 1944-45. Charles Scribner's Sons. New York.
- Blumenson, Martin. Breakout and Pursuit. Washington. 1961.
- Bradley, Omar. A Soldier's Story. London. 1952
- Bradley, Omar. A General's life. New York. 1982.
- Bryant, Arthur. The Turn of the Tide. London. 1957
- Bryant, Arthur. Triumph in the West. London. 1959.
- Bryant, Arthur. The Great Duke. Collins. 1971.
- Burton, Graham. Air Battles. Marshall Cavendish Publishing Ltd. London. 1974.
- Butcher Captain H. C. My Three Years Eisenhower. London. 1946.
- Butler, J. R. M. & Gwyer, M. A. Grand Strategy. Vol III. London. 1964.
- Carver, Lt Col R.M.P. Second to None, The Royal Scots Greys, 1919-1945. Messrs McCorquodale & Co Ltd. 1954.
- Carver, Michael. Out of Step. Hutchinson. 1989.

- Carell, Paul. Invasion -They're coming!. George G. Harrap & Co Ltd. 1962.
- Cassidy, G. L. Warpath. The Story of the Algonquin Regiment, 1939-1945. The Ryerson Press. Toronto. 1948.
- Chalfont, Alun. Montgomery, of Alamein. London. 1976.
- Chant, Christopher. Preston, Anthony. Shaw, Jenny. World War II. Sundial Books Ltd. London. 1979.
- Churchill, Winston. Triumph and Tragedy. London. 1954.
- Collins, J. Lawton. Lightning Joe. Louisiana. 1979.
- Cooper, Matthew. The German Army: Its Political and Military Failure. London. 1978.
- Copp, Terry. & Vogel, Robert. Maple Leaf Route: Falaise. Maple Leaf Route. Ontario. 1983.
- Craven & Cate. The U. S. Army Air Forces in World War II. Chicago. 1951.
- Cruikshank, Charles. Deception in World War II. Oxford. 1979.
- Darman, Peter. Uniforms of World War II. Brown Packaging Books Ltd. London. 1998.
- De Guingand, Frederick. Operation Victory. London. 1960.
- Delaforce, Patrick. The Polar Bears. Alan Sutton Publishing Ltd. 1995.
- D'Este, Carlo. Decision in Normandy. HarperCollins. 1983.
- Dugdale & Wood. Complete Orders of Battle of the Waffen-SS in Normandy, Vol I. Books International. 1997.
- Dunn, Walter Scott. Second Front Now -1943. Alabama. 1980.
- Dupuy, Colonel T. N. A Genius for War. London. 1977.
- Edwards, Roger. Panzer. A Revolution in Warfare 1939-1945. Arms and Armor Press. Ltd. 1989.
- Ehreman, John. Grand Strategy, Vol. V. London. 1956.
- Eisenhower, David. Eisenhower at War 1943-1945. Random House. 1986.
- Eisenhower, Dwight. Crusade in Europe. New York. 1948.
- Eisenhower, Dwight. Papers, Vol. III. Baltimore. 1970.

- Ellis, Chris. Tanks of World War 2. Octopus Books Ltd. 1981.
- Ellis, L. Victory in the West, Vol I. The Battle of Normandy. H M Stationery Office. 1962.
- Farago, Ladislas, Patton. Ordeal and Triumph. New York. 1963.
- Farrar-Hockley, Anthony. Infantry Tactics 1939-45. London. 1976.
- Featherston, Alwyn. Saving the Breakout. Presido Press. USA. 1993.
- Fergusson, Bernard. The Black Watch and The King's Enemies. London. 1950.
- Fergusson, Bernard. The Watery Maze. London. 1961.
- Foot, M. R. D. SOE in France. London. 1966.
- Ford, Roger. The Tiger Tank. Brown Packaging Books Ltd. London. 1998.
- Forty, George. Desert Rats at War. Ian Allan. London. 1977.
- Forty, George. German Tanks of World War II. Arms and Armour Press. London. 1987.
- Foss, Christopher. Tanks and Fighting Vehicles. Salamander Books Ltd. London. 1977.
- Foster, Tony. Meeting of Generals. Methuen. Canada. 1986.
- Fraser, Sir David. And We Shall Shock Them. London. 1983.
- Fraser, Sir David. Alanbrooke. London. 1982.
- Gavin, James. On To Berlin. London. 1978.
- Golley, John. The Big Drop. London. 1982.
- Gosset & Lecomte. Caen Pendant La Bataille. Caen. 1946.
- Greenfield, Palmer & Wiley. The U. S. Army in World War II, The Organization of Ground Combat Troops. Washington. 1946.
- Grigg, John. 1943: The Victory that Never Was. London. 1980.
- Guderian, Heinz. Panzer Leader. London. 1952.
- Gudgin, Peter. Armoured Firepower. Sutton Publishing Ltd. Gloucester. 1997.
- Hamilton, Nigel. Montgomery: The Making of a General. London. 1981.

- Hamilton, Nigel. Montgomery: Master of a Battlefield. London. 1983.
- Hammerton, John. The Second Great War, Volumes I,II,IV & VI. The Waverly Book Co. Ltd. London.
- Harrison, Gordon. Cross Channel Attack. Washington. 1951.
- Hart, Sir Basil Liddell. History of the Second World War. Octopus Books Ltd. London. 1974.
- Hart Dyke, Trevor. Normandy to Arnhem. 4th Bn Yorkshire Volunteers. 1966.
- Hastings, Max. Bomber Command. London. 1979.
- Hastings, Max. Das Reich. London. 1982.
- Hastings, Max. Overlord. Macmillan Publishing Ltd.   Oxford. 1999.
- Hastings, R. The Rifle Brigade 1939-1945. Gale & Polden. 1950.
- Haswell, J. The Intelligence and Deception of the D-Day Landings. London. 1979.
- Haupt, Werner. Army Group Centre. Schiffer Publishing Ltd. USA. 1998.
- Haupt, Werner. Army Group North. Schiffer Publishing Ltd. USA. 1998.
- Haupt, Werner. Army Group South. Schiffer Publishing Ltd. USA. 1998.
- Hewitt, Robert. Workhorse of the Western Front. Washington Infantry Journal Press. 1946.
- Hinsley, Prof. F H. & others. British Intelligence in the Second World War, Vol II. London. 1981.
- Hogg, Ian. The Guns of World War II. Macdonald & Jane's. 1976.
- How, J. J. Normandy; The British Breakout. London. 1981.
- How, Major J. J. MC. Hill 112-Cornerstone of the Normandy Campaign. William Kimber & Co Ltd. 1984.
- Howard, Michael. Grand Strategy, Vol. IV. London. 1972.
- Howarth, David. Dawn of D-Day. London. 1959.
- Hunt, Robert & Hartman, Tom. Swastika At War. Ebenezer Baylis and Son Ltd. London 1975.

- Irving, David. Hitler's War. London & New York. 1979.
- Irving, David. The Trail of the Fox. London & New York. 1977.
- Irving, David. The Rise and Fall of the Luftwaffe. Boston. 1973.
- Ismay, Lord. Memoirs. London. 1960.
- Joly, Cyril. Take These Men. London. 1955.
- Jonson, G, & Dunphie, C. Brightly Shone the Dawn. London. 1980.
- Keeble, Lewis. Worm's Eye View-The Recollections of Lewis Keeble. Appx C to 'Battlefield Tour, 1st/4th KOYLI in the NW Europe Campaign' by Geoffrey Barker-Harland.
- Keegan, John. Six Armies in Normandy. Jonathan Cape. 1982.
- Keegan, John. Who was who in World War II. Arms and Armour Press. London. 1978.
- Kohn & Harahan (eds). Air Superiority in World War II and Korea. Washington. 1983.
- Kurowski. Panzer Aces. J.J. Fedorowicz Publishing Inc. Canada. 1992.
- Lamb, Richard. Montgomery in Europe. London. 1983.
- Lane, Ronald L. Rudder's Rangers. Manassas. 1979.
- Lefevre, Eric. Panzers in Normandy, Then and Now. 'After the Battle' Magazine. 1983.
- Lehmann, Rudolf. The Leibstandarte Parts I, II and III. J. J. Fedorowicz Publishing Inc. Manitoba. Canada. 1987, 1988, 1990.
- Lehmann, Rudolf & Tiemann, Ralf, The Leibstandarte IV/I. J. J. Fedorowicz Publishing Inc. Manitoba. Canada. 1993.
- Lewin, Ronald. Montgomery as Military Commander. London. 1971.
- Lewin, Ronald. Ultra Goes to War. London. 1978.
- Liddell Hart, Basil. The Other Side of the Hill. London. 1951.
- Liddell Hart, Basil. The Second World War. London. 1970.
- Lindsay and Johnson. History of the 7th Armoured Division 1943-45. Unpublished. 1945. Author's possession.
- Lovat, Lord. March Past. London. 1978.

- Lucas, James. Das Reich. Cassell. 1991.
- Lucas, James & Barker, James. The Killing Ground. B. T. Batsford. 1978.
- Luck, Hans von. Panzer Commander. Praeger. New York. 1989.
- Macksey, Kenneth. Armoured Crusader. London. 1967.
- Maczek, Stanislaw. Avec Mes Blindês. Presses de la Citê. Paris.
- Martin, H. G. The History of the 15th Scottish Division 1939-1945. William Blackwood & Sons Ltd. 1948.
- Maule, Henry. Caen: The Brutal Battle and the Break-out from Normandy. London. 1976.
- Marshall, S. L. A. Night Drop. London. 1962.
- McBryde, Brenda. A Nurse's War. London. 1979.
- McKee, Alexander. Caen, Anvil of Victory. London. 1964.
- Messenger, Charles. Hitler's Gladiator. Brassey's. 1988.
- Messenger, Charles. The Pictorial History of World War II. Bison Books Ltd. London. 1987.
- Meyer, Hubert. History of the 12th SS Panzer Division Hitlerjugend. J. J. Fedorowicz Publishing Inc, Manitoba. Canada. 1994.
- Meyer, Kurt. Grenadiers. J. J. Fedorowicz Publishing Inc. Manitoba. Canada. 1994.
- Montgomery, B. L. Memoirs of Field Marshal the Viscount Montgomery. HarperCollins. 1958.
- Moorehead, Alan. Montgomery. London. 1947.
- Morgan, F. E. Overture to Overlord. London. 1950.
- Neillands, Robin. The Desert Rats. Weidenfeld and Nicolson. London.
- Nicolson, N. Alex. Weidenfeld & Nicolson. 1973.
- Nelson. Second Front Now-1943. Alabama. 1980.
- Palmer, Wiley & Keast. The U. S. Army in World War II: The Procurement and Training of Ground Combat Troops. Washington. 1948.
- Patton, George S. War as I Knew it. Boston. 1947.

- Pogue, Forrest C. George C. Marshall, Vols II & III, New York. 1965, 1973.
- Preston, Anthony. Decisive Battles of Hitler's War. New Brulington Books. London. 1977.
- Price, Alford. Spick, Mike. Great Aircraft of World War II. Abbeydale Press. Ltd. 1997.
- Readers Digest. The World at Arms. The Readers Digest Association Ltd. London. 1989.
- Renolds, Michael. Steel Inferno. Spellmount. Staplehurst. 1997.
- Rhodes, Anthony. Propaganda. The Art of Persuasion in World War II. The Wellfleet Press. 1987. London.
- Ritgen, Helmut. Die Geschichte der Panzer Lehr Division im Western 1944-1945. Motorbuch Verlag. Stuttgart. 1979.
- Roach, Peter. The 8.15 to War. London. 1982.
- Rohmer, Richard. Patton's Gap. London. 1981.
- Ross, George MacLeod. The Business of Tanks. London (privately printed). 1976.
- Ruge, Frederich. Rommel in Normandy. London. 1979.
- Ruppenthal, Ronald G. The U. S. Army In World War II. Logistical Support of the Armies. Washington. 1966.
- Ryan, Cornelius. The Longest Day. London & New York. 1959.
- Sayer, Ian and Botting, Douglas. Hitler's Last General. Bantam Press 1989.
- Scarfe, Norman. Assault Division. London. 1947.
- Scott, Desmond. Typhoon Pilot. London. 1982.
- Seaton, Albert. The Fall of Fortress Europe 1943-45. London. 1981.
- Seaton, Albert. The German Army. London. 1982.
- Shulman, Milton. Defeat in the West. Masquerade. 1995.
- Spearhead in the West. The Third Armored Division 1941-45. Turner Publishing Co. USA.
- Speidel, Hans. We Defended Normandy. London. 1951.
- Stacey, C. P. Col. Official History of the Canadian Army in the Second World War, Vol III,

- The Victory Campaign. Queen's Printer. Ottawa. Canada. 1960.
- Strong, Kenneth. Intelligence at the Top. London. 1968.
- Tedder, Lord. With Prejudice. London. 1966
- Van Creveld, Martin. Supplying War. London. 1978.
- Van Creveld, Martin. Fighting Power: German Military Performance 1914-45. Washington. 1980.
- Vannoy, Allyn R. and Karamales, Jay. Against The Panzers. McFarland & Co. 1996.
- Verney, G. L. The Desert Rats. Greenhill Books. 1990.
- Warlimont, Walter. Inside Hitler's Headquarters. London. 1962.
- Webster & Frankland. The Strategic Air Offensive Against Germany, Vol. III. London. 1961.
- Weigley, Russell F. Eisenhower's Lieutenants. London & New York. 1980.
- Weller, Jac. Weapons and Tactics: Hastings to Berlin. New York. 1966.
- West, Nigel. MI6: British Secret Intelligence Service Operations 1909-45. London. 1983.
- Westphal, S. The German Army in the West. London. 1951.
- When all our brothers are Silent. Association of Soldiers of the Former Waffen-SS. Verlag Munin. Osnabrueck. 1981.
- Wilmot, Chester. The Struggle for Europe. HarperCollins. 1952.
- Wilson, Andrew. Flamethrower. London. 1974.
- Woolcombe, Robert. Lion Rampant. London. 1970.
- Young, Brigadier Peter. World War II. Tiger Books International Ltd. London. 1980.

MORE FROM THE SAME SERIES

Most books from the 'World War II from Original Sources' series are edited and endorsed by Emmy Award winning film maker and military historian Bob Carruthers, producer of Discovery Channel's Line of Fire and Weapons of War and BBC's Both Sides of the Line. Long experience and strong editorial control gives the military history enthusiast the ability to buy with confidence.

The series advisor is David McWhinnie, producer of the acclaimed Battlefield series for Discovery Channel. David and Bob have co-produced books and films with a wide variety of the UK's leading historians including Professor John Erickson and Dr David Chandler.

Where possible the books draw on rare primary sources to give the military enthusiast new insights into a fascinating subject.

For more information visit www.pen-and-sword.co.uk